MW00695438

CUTTING
THE TIES OF KARMA

CUTTING
_{THE} TIES OF KARMA

Understanding the Patchwork
of Your Past Lives

Phyllis Krystal

⊕ WEISER BOOKS
York Beach, Maine, USA

First published in 2001 by
Weiser Books, Inc.
P.O. Box 612
York Beach, ME 03910-0612
www.weiserbooks.com

Library of Congress Cataloging-in-Publication Data

Krystal, Phyllis.
    Cutting the ties of karma : understanding the patchwork of your past lives /
Phyllis Krystal.
        p.   cm.
    Includes index.
    ISBN 1-57863-224-2 (pbk. : alk. paper)
    1. Spiritual life.   2. Karma.   I. Title.
  BL624.K79   2001
  291.4'46—dc21   00–068530

Typeset in Minion, with Lithos Bold display

Cover design by Ed Stevens

Printed in the United States of America

08 07 06 05 04 03 02 01
8   7   6   5   4   3   2   1

The paper used in this publication meets the minimum requirements of the
American National Standard for Information Sciences—Permanence of Paper
for Printed Library Materials Z39.48-1992 (R1997).

I dedicate this book to Sri Sathya Sai Baba who, by his presence in the world at this time, can help us remove many patches that we have yet to release so we can be free from their control over us.

Contents

PART IV
FAMILY KARMA

PART V
PATCHES OF KARMA

EXERCISES

Acknowledgments

First, I would like to thank the Hi C within everyone with whom I have worked for the helpful contributions to this work. I am grateful to Peggy Lenney for the help she has given me to bring this book to light. And, most of all, my heartfelt thanks to Sathya Sai Baba for his continued encouragement and support of my work.

INTRODUCTION

This book will explain the various lessons we must learn in this life if we failed to learn them in previous ones. It will incorporate some of the symbols and exercises presented in *Cutting the Ties That Bind*, *Cutting More Ties That Bind* and the *Cutting the Ties That Bind Workbook*. In the latter, the symbols are illustrated and the exercises are outlined in simple steps that make it possible for anyone—even children—to follow. It is therefore advisable to work with these books before undertaking the work contained in this one, which is on a deeper level.

My basic goal is to provide help and instruction for people who are interested and willing to use the work to gain freedom from outer controls, such as dominating people, habits, or addictions, and from anyone or anything in whom we seek security. The freedom thus achieved allows us to be guided by the Hi C, the only truly reliable inner source of wisdom, a source that is available to everyone. In this way we can become Its instruments instead of remaining controlled by our own limited ego.

PART I
KARMA AND YOU

Chapter 1

What Is a Patchwork Quilt?

When the outline for this book first came to my mind it was a real surprise. The insight I received was that we are all born into each new life wearing a patchwork quilt that is composed of many different pieces, all brought over from past lives. I was intrigued with this idea, yet I questioned its validity. Only after much pondering on my part was I able to understand its significance.

Patchwork, according to Webster's dictionary, is "anything formed of irregular, incongruous, odd or miscellaneous parts, such as a quilt made of odd patches of cloth sewn together at the edge." This definition took me back to childhood memories of growing up in England around the beginning of the 20th century. I remember hearing about groups of women who met regularly for quilting "bees." These gatherings usually took place during the daytime while children were in school. They served as a social function, for the women could chat, exchange recipes, enjoy tea and pastries, and above all, relax from the daily role of wife and mother.

Originally, quilts were fashioned from small scraps of material salvaged from old clothing. The material used for the patches had, at some previous time, been part of some article of clothing. But over the years the cloth disintegrates with wear and cleaning, and is obviously worn out. The wear and tear is usually more pronounced in some areas of a piece of clothing than in other parts. Only those parts that are still usable are salvaged when the garment can no longer be worn. These "still good" parts are combined with other pieces to make a quilt that can be used to cover a bed and keep someone warm at night.

In the past people didn't have as much clothing as we have today, and it was the custom to find new uses for clothes that were no longer wearable. People were far more conscious of waste than is now the case. In many families, clothes had already been patched and darned to extend their "life," or they were cut down to a smaller size to fit younger family members. When I attended school in England, girls were required to take classes to learn sewing, knitting, and dressmaking. In addition, we learned how to patch and darn to prolong the life of clothing showing signs of wear. This practice was taken for granted, and no one looked down on anyone wearing mended clothes. In fact, mothers were applauded for being frugal.

Nowadays there is such a proliferation of merchandise available that people are tempted to buy whatever they see displayed in stores, or advertised in the media, particularly on television and the Internet, whether they need new clothes or not. Obsolescence is accepted because it allows people to indulge in shopping for something new and different without considering whether they really need it, or even if they can afford it. People are also seduced into discarding the old and investing in ever-new clothes in order to "keep up with the Jones's," who are busy doing the same thing themselves, either to impress others or to gain a false sense of security by wearing only the very latest fashions.

So our patchwork quilt originated from a frugal practice. When the old garment was ready to be discarded, the good pieces of cloth were cut into small pieces and saved until there was enough to fit and sew together to make a quilt. The work involved fitting all the pieces together and making an attractive pattern. It was both time-consuming and tedious when undertaken alone, so the "quilting bee" came into being. An added advantage to the social function was that some of the women could exchange cloth, which provided more variety for each of their quilts.

Only the pieces of cloth that still had some "life" left in them were used for the quilt. And, symbolically, we can imagine that each human being wears a patchwork quilt composed of many small irregularly shaped parts, each one salvaged from the many worn-out "garments" representing various personalities from past lives. Each small piece (or personality part) has been brought over from the past as a remnant that still has some "life" in it. But each piece is now being used differently, as it is only a small part of a new quilt, rather than being a whole article.

In dreams, clothes often represent attitudes or behavior, so we could think of our individual patchwork quilt as a coat of many colors, just like the one Joseph had in the biblical story, much to his brothers' distaste and envy. Our patchwork quilts are the sum total of many attitudes and behaviors we bring with us from the past.

Some of the "coats" we wear are attractive and cause others to be envious, while others are so tattered and torn that their wearer is despised and dismissed as being worthless. But we have been taught in this reverie work that neither the outer garment nor the body is the true identity. Whether or not it appears to be ugly or beautiful, it merely represents the package or container, the house or temple containing the Real Self.

To take this idea further: in order to produce cloth the material is woven on some kind of a loom. According to the encyclopedia, "weaving is the art of forming fabric by interlacing at right angles two sets of yarn or other material. The loom is a frame, usually made of wood on which the warp threads are firmly secured. A shuttle carries the woof and is used to pass the thread in and out of the warp to form the fabric."

So each patch is composed of two sets of threads woven at right angles to one another to form the cloth. The warp can be likened to all the past tendencies, actions, habits, and reactions that still contain energy or life. The woof would be all the conditions, family, friends, and experiences that are magnetically drawn to each of us. They can enable us in the present life to work out whatever is needed to expend the energy that still remains in each patch from the past. When the woof is removed, the warp falls away. When the task is accomplished, the patch can be discarded. When the lesson is learned, the situation that was necessary to teach it is removed.

We all tend to follow old patterns. We often continue to fear the worst and thus attract to us the gloom and doom we expect. In this way, once such a habit is established, a vicious circle continues to operate. This book is about discovering the habits that we can change, and we can use the exercises mentioned in the text to help us remove habits we want to replace.

CHAPTER 2

WHO OR WHAT IS THE HI C?

I WILL BE USING THE term Hi C to refer to High Self or Higher Consciousness throughout this book. I am often asked, "What is the Hi C?" Actually, there is no definitive answer. We cannot pin down such an abstract concept in a futile effort to render it more tangible or understandable as we would pin down a butterfly in order to examine it. It will always be as a will-of-the-wisp—just out of reach and beyond our control.

Over the centuries, the Hi C has been compared to a flame or a lamp hidden deep within every living creature. A diamond or pearl, or other precious stones, as well as gold, have also been used to refer to It. It has been called the Christ Self, the Buddha Self, the Atma, the Baba Self, the High Self or Higher Consciousness. The latter was the inspiration for the term Hi C that I use in my work, being the initials for Higher Consciousness.

But all of these words are merely different appellations referring to the same entity, which remains out of reach of any name or attempted description. So how can we define the Hi C?

In my work I have been taught to withdraw my attention from the outer scene and direct it within myself to be taught by the Hi C which is available within every living person. It is that part of each one of us that never dies. It is eternal and cannot be damaged or affected in any way. It is the Real Self that incarnates during each sojourn on Earth by entering a baby's body that has been prepared as Its temporary home or residence for this lifetime. It is fully aware of what still needs to be learned and how each new birth presents an opportunity to do so.

It has gathered around itself—during numerous entries into physical form—many attributes, some positive, but many negative. In so doing, a separation has occurred, as the body/mind/ego/personality sheath assumes control and acts apart from the direction of the Hi C, even to the extent of being completely unaware of Its existence, and identifying solely with the container. I distinctly recall one time when my late husband and I were called for an interview by Sathya Sai Baba. As we were all seated on the floor waiting for him to enter the interview room, he glided into the room with a big smile at what he was about to say. He then announced to the gathering, "Did you know that you are all walking temples?" We were all highly amused and I, for one, realized that I had never thought of such an apt description, but recognized at once how very pertinent it was. Of course, the body/mind complex is the temple in which resides the God Self which is our Reality. So we need to make sure that our temple is kept clean, both inside and outside, to provide a suitable place to worship the Real Self and eventually merge with It.

To further impress this message more deeply, in another interview, Baba informed us that we are not sinners but gods. He then turned to me, and with an intense and penetrating gaze and stern voice, said, "Mrs. Krystal, say 'I am God.'" I was not only startled, but positively horrified! I had been brought up in the Church of England tradition and would have been severely punished had I dared to utter what would have been deemed a sacrilege. So all I managed to say was, "I cannot." But Baba would not accept that and persisted by saying, "Say it." So I tried to obey, but all that came out of my mouth was a mere whisper that did not satisfy him, so he again demanded that I say it. I finally summoned up enough courage to say the frightening words, only to be told, "Louder," so I repeated them several times until he was satisfied. By insisting in this way, Baba was trying to teach me my true identity, and at the same time, demonstrate to the others in the interview the same lesson, that we are all God and will finally merge with that Real Self when we have allowed It to use us as Its instruments so that our will and Its will are one and the same, and not separate.

It is as if It projects Itself outside of Itself to experience the world, and, in so doing, becomes more aware of Itself. But many people ask how they can get in touch with the Hi C once they have accepted Its existence. To make contact with It, I offer the Maypole Exercise.

Exercise 1
USING THE MAYPOLE

To practice the Maypole Exercise, visualize or imagine a maypole consisting of a long pole set upright in front of you. To the top of it are attached many ribbons of all the colors of a rainbow, hanging down all around it. Each ribbon can be used as a telephone connection to the Hi C, which is visualized at the top of the maypole. The Hi C (or superconscious) is projected up high and above the conscious mind, as opposed to the subconscious, which is below or beneath the level of conscious thought.

Imagine you are taking a ribbon of any color that appeals to you and using it as you would a telephone. Ask the Hi C to supply you with whatever It knows you need, since It knows better than you do exactly what that is. Place your hands in your lap (open like bowls) ready to receive from the Hi C.

Many people complain of feeling tense and nervous, so ask to be given relaxing energy via your ribbon. Breathe it in and let go of tension as you breathe out. Ask for healing energy, which you then inhale; and exhale any condition that causes you unease or distress, whether physical, mental, or emotional. Next, ask for cleansing energy to remove any negative thoughts, feelings, or memories as you allow them to flow out with your breath. Many people say that they want to do something, but they cannot seem to summon up sufficient strength to follow through with action. So breathe in strengthening energy, and exhale any weakness you are willing to release. Lastly, ask for the special kind of love that can be supplied only by the Hi C. This love is not limited or selfish as human love so often tends to be. Breathe in this completely fulfilling love—deeply but gently—and breathe out any obstacles to receiving it, such as guilt, a low self-image, or anything else that could prevent you from accepting it. It is your birthright, which you do not have to deserve or earn, but merely request and breathe in.

As it begins to circulate within you, open your heart to receive it. It is completely safe to do so, as it will never cause you pain or rejection, but can fulfill your deepest need. To make it easier to open your heart, imagine a flower in your heart. Check it to see if it is open or closed in a tight bud. If the latter is the case, command it to open up sufficiently to allow the love from the Hi C to penetrate it, just as an actual flower opens up to receive the sunlight.

Imagine the love flowing in to fill all the empty spaces so many of us carry with us all our lives. To keep the love flowing it needs an outlet. If you clutch it too tightly and selfishly, it will gradually have a negative and opposite effect and will also block the flow from the Hi C. To prevent this from happening, invite anyone who comes to your mind who needs this love, to share it. Those people who are difficult or negative, or those with whom you have a problem or an unpleasant relationship are in great need of this kind of love, or they would not be so negative. So make sure you invite them with the rest of the invisible guests. In order to send love to others, simply place your palms together (with fingers extended) and point them to each person you have invited to participate. You do not have to love or even like these people, but you will find that if you practice this exercise regularly, the most difficult relationships will improve.

Many people feel helpless as individuals to bring about even very obvious and essential changes in the world situation. This need not be the case, for people can join with an ever-increasing number of others in numerous countries, who are practicing this way by directing love to other parts of the world where it is lacking.

To join this growing multitude, extend this love to groups of people who are lonely, sick, depressed, or acutely in need of help, such as the inhabitants of prisons, insane asylums, orphanages, hospitals, senior citizens' homes, refugee camps, and any other group that comes to your mind when you ask to be shown where you can direct it. Then it should be sent to those countries where there is warfare, famine, sickness, hunger, oppression, torture, or other conditions that create suffering for those caught in such misery. In addition, the heads of the various countries certainly need to be more loving in their positions of authority over the peoples' lives, so send love to them, too, for they can then bring about necessary changes.

I am repeatedly being informed of the small miracles that are becoming an almost daily occurrence in many parts of the world, wherever people are using this simple daily ritual. For instance, in Russia a regular program has been launched whereby those who have been exposed to this technique put aside a few minutes every Thursday evening at seven o'clock Russian time, to direct the love wherever people are in need of it. They report that it first begins to bring about a change in their own attitude, then in their family members, in their co-workers and out into their own country and to the rest of the world. It is a very simple exercise that requires only a small expenditure of time to practice, but it can have a worldwide effect.

Since the problems in the world all stem from the same primary cause—the absence of heart and the expression of love—both aspects of yin, or feminine, receptive energy, we want to help bring about a balance between yin and yang (the more aggressive masculine energy which is so dominant in the world). By being willing to direct this love to all with whom we come in contact, and all who are suffering from lack of it, we can make a difference.

CHAPTER 3

WHO ARE YOU?
WHO AM I?

I HAVE BEEN TAUGHT
that at the Hi C level, we are all one—and furthermore—we
are all equal. No one is either better or less worthy than
anyone else. So why is there such disparity between people
and what causes the apparent inequality? We have also been
taught that each personality is the sum total of many different influences, not only in this present life but also brought
over from many lifetimes in the past.

It reminds me of the way identical diamonds could be
wrapped in different packages, some of which are very
beautiful, others unattractive. Are the diamonds in the drab
packages any less valuable than those in the more colorful
wrappings? All are of equal value. We are deceived only by
the outer package. No one can guess what is inside a parcel
until the outer covering is removed and the contents revealed. Some packages are tightly wrapped, even hermeti-
cally sealed, and it may involve hard work to open them up
to discover the contents. The same is true for each of us. We
have been programmed to identify with the outer package

or container, composed of the body-mind-ego-personality and we often overlook the fact that concealed within this container is the Hi C.

However, we need these containers or receptacles to enable us to live in the world and to learn how to break the karma we have all set in motion. Only when we enter a new physical body at birth are we given another chance to detach from old inappropriate behavior and learn new ways of interacting with others whom we meet along the way on our journey from birth to death. Whatever we sent out into the world or to other people at any time can only be adjusted while we are in a physical body living in the world. Then we can remedy past mistakes and learn necessary lessons. The encouraging fact is that we have brought with us into each new life exactly what we need to help us to undertake the task for which we have re-entered the world.

I recall one particular time while in a reverie (or waking dream) I was shown the long involved path of evolution we have all been traveling, though mostly unconsciously, for many lifetimes. On that occasion Baba appeared on my inner screen as soon as I had relaxed and closed my eyes in readiness to concentrate on whatever messages or insights would be forthcoming during the session.

The first thing that came to me was as if Baba were saying, "I want to show you all the people who have ever lived in the world." I was quite taken back at such a prospect. Baba swept out his right arm in a wide arc toward the sky and indicated what looked like millions of tiny stars or sparks of light. He then proceeded to explain that everyone who has ever lived in the world has embarked on a journey toward the eventual goal of union with the Real Self. Unfortunately, most people are not aware of this fact and are living their lives blindly, following their senses which, in turn, attach them to the demands of the body and the outer world. He referred to this process as the slow and gradual way of evolution. It is a hit or miss way undertaken on an unconscious level by the vast majority of people. He next announced that he would show me those people who had broken free from this slow process and were conscious of the reason for human birth, which is to become free from all attachments to the tangible world and to be ready and willing to move ahead more rapidly. He then moved his arm in a wide arc on the opposite side and I became aware of similar bright lights, like stars, but far fewer in number than the first ones he showed me. He continued to explain that these represented those souls who, having broken free from all attachments, were Self-motivated.

He then showed me that there was a gap or crevasse dividing the two sets of lights, and this crevasse had to be crossed. Only when all attachments, or what Baba refers to as excess baggage, are released can that gulf be crossed because the baggage weighs too much for us to be able to make the leap if we continue to hold onto our "stuff."

Interestingly enough, this present time in which we have been born can further our release more rapidly due to the acceleration of all aspects of life as we move into this new century. The quickening pace can overwhelm us. Or it can propel us forward, for the increased momentum helps us apply ourselves with extra dedication to the task. We can harness ourselves to this increased energy and move ahead, or we can give up hope and allow it to overpower us. It is our decision and no one can make it for us. It requires self-observation, but in addition, it also requires the absence of harsh self-criticism or self-flagellation, for both habits are wasteful and lead nowhere.

We all need to consult our own individual map to learn the specific areas that must be addressed. We are all magnetically attracted to birth into a particular family composed of the various members already in it, together with the heritage including nationality, race, country, and so forth.

At the birth of my first child, I remember commenting that it would be so helpful if babies arrived complete with instructions, like those provided with the various household appliances we use daily—from electric toothbrushes, all the kitchen appliances, to cars and more complex instruments. Now, I realize that we do come into each new life with a full set of helpful hints, but we need to be detectives to unravel their meaning and then use them to help us attain our full potential.

We enter life with a contract to fulfill, and it is up to each of us how we handle it. If it is not accepted and completed, we will have another opportunity at some future time when the circumstances allow it. But all of our contracts must be completed since we have ourselves incurred them.

What do we bring with us into each new life to form the patchwork quilt? Even more important, what tools are available to help us to work on the various patches that are still active from the past?

In this computer age it is easy to understand the answer to these questions. We can visualize each person being born complete with a computer programmed to attract those experiences, events, people, and relationships that enable us to complete some of the unfinished business from past lives. There are as many different computers as there are people, and the remarkable fact is that there are no two alike. This is true for members of the same family and even for identical twins. Each computer is specifically programmed according to the personal past history throughout many sojourns on Earth. For instance, it is a well-known fact that no two people have identical fingerprints and this variation holds true for every other part of the human form. It is indeed mind-boggling to consider the vast variety of individual characteristics in human beings. Each person has a unique karmic history, part of which is brought in at each birth. Not every influence from past lives can be worked on in the present one, only those for which this life was designed. In addition, in the current life, we are once again creating karma that will need to be addressed at some time in the future when the circumstances allow us to do so. Only if we decide to let the Hi C use us as Its instrument can we avoid accruing karmic debts that will have to be paid off at an appropriate time in the future.

We are given limited choice. We are free to decide what attitude to assume. That will determine to what extent we can take advantage of any opportunity we are given. We can learn from the many diverse aspects of our lives or ignore this gift. If we ignore it, we lose a chance to detach from past actions, and we will not be free to allow the light within to express in everything we think, feel, say, or do, and which could ultimately lead to freedom from our ego control.

Everyone and everything in the manifest world is imperfect or flawed. Only the Real Self is perfect. It has been the custom in many cultures for artists to make a deliberate mistake in a piece of handiwork, because it was believed that only God is capable of making anything perfect.

We have defects—as well as positive attributes—and many of us try to cover up our defects. We pretend—both to ourselves and to others—that we are perfect, but that attitude is not conducive to growth or wholeness. Only when we are willing to admit to our faults, or blemishes, can we start to correct or erase them, and then we are able to advance. So instead of being defensive about our negative aspects, we need to admit to them, for when we do so we will be able to change.

CHAPTER 4

MYTHS

I THINK THE TIME IS right to explode some myths. Myths tend to develop around certain people, or are projected onto them by others. The myth often has very little connection to the person who is thus forced to assume it. It is composed of the qualities that other people want to see in someone else and are a projection of their own desires. In this way the mythic person carries for such people their own dreams, so that they are able to live vicariously through their idol. However, it is very hard for the individual who is thus forced to carry the myth, and who is required to live out the expectations of all his or her admirers. These erstwhile fans can just as easily turn against the person who falls short of their expectations, so it becomes necessary to live two separate lives, one public and the other private. Rarely do the two coincide. This situation sometimes results in a schizoid condition. In some cases the outer or public image gains so much control that it takes over the person's life and drowns out any personal life he or she may originally have led. In many cases the pressure becomes too intense, and the person breaks down under the strain, or escapes by using drugs or alcohol to try to alleviate the unbearable stress imposed by the role.

In addition to the problems the myth causes to the recipient of the unwanted role, it also causes problems for the various people who have expected someone else to live out their dreams instead of living their own life more fully. So both the idolized figure and his or her worshipers suffer from the myth phenomenon. How can one person live out the dreams of many people when these dreams are all so different? It creates an intolerable situation for the one and great disappointment for the many. If the public figure is an example or a role model for others, and can also live out his or her own life to the fullest extent, then many others can benefit from this example. The most serious effect of hero worship is that it involves attachment to a figure outside and separate from the person on whom expectations are being projected. Any such attachment prevents people from relying solely on the inner core of their own being, the Hi C.

To my own consternation, I have lately begun to realize that a myth has been growing around my life, and this myth obscures the truth of who I am and what I do. Most of it is so far from the truth that I am amazed! For instance, some people believe that I live a very glamorous and exciting life because I travel frequently to many different parts of the world. In their minds I am doing all those things they wish they could do. Some are deriving a vicarious thrill from it, while others are perhaps a bit jealous or envious, wishing they were in my shoes.

Actually, I do travel a great deal, but I travel to teach. I usually see the airport and the scenery from there to the hotel where I will be staying, unless I arrive at night, when it is too dark to see anything. Later, I see the hotel and my room and whatever scenery lies on the way to the hall where I will be giving seminars the following morning. Other than these locations, I usually see very little of the cities where I go to carry out my work. Sightseeing is rarely possible except on a few occasions, since the time between seminars is generally used for travel to the next location. There is also the travel itself, which can be exhausting, especially at my age. Since my husband died, I travel alone by choice, which means I am obliged to take care of all the practical details, such as airline tickets, passport, visa, currency exchange, luggage and all the other important, though seemingly insignificant, details involved with travel to foreign countries. Then there is the effect of jetlag when travel involves flying through several time zones. Food and water can prove to be hazardous, and quick changes of climate require time for adjusting the body. So, all in all, travel is not always as glamorous as it might appear, especially in recent times when there has been such a tremendous increase in the number of people moving from one part of the world to another. As with everything, there is always a price to pay.

Another mistaken belief is that I am "close to Baba," as people are apt to express it. That, too, is another fallacy. Baba himself says that no one is closer to him than any other, for we are all equal in his eyes. But he is able to see below the surface of our personality, so he knows which of us is ready to be used as his instruments. Once that process begins, we are forced to let go of all the varied desires we may cherish and be willing to be used in whatever way necessary, whether we like it or not. As Baba says, "Don't do only what you like, but like what you have to do." So again, there is a price to pay for the apparent closeness to Baba. In addition, he is a stern taskmaster, and once we have made the decision to allow him to use us, we have to be prepared, to "love my uncertainty," as he expresses it, and be willing to change plans instantly if that becomes necessary.

Those people who find themselves in the public eye are faced with a difficult task; that of maintaining their own identity and integrity, in spite of all the expectations from a multitude of sources and innumerable people, the vast majority of whom are unknown to them. The only way I have found to deal with a minor version of this situation is to take time to withdraw my attention from the outer world, with all its demands, to focus on the inner dweller, the only real guide who is always utterly reliable. Added to that regular daily exercise, every morning I ask the Hi C to think, feel, speak, act, and love through me all day. In this way I find that It can increasingly be the motivator. As that gradually becomes more and more a reality, a certain detachment begins to develop, whereby the results of the actions are no longer connected to the small personality, but to the Hi C as the originator, with the small self as the instrument in Its hands. This can free each person from the burden imposed by all the outer pressures from the various situations and people with their own selfish motives.

Each one of us is, first and foremost, responsible only for the way we conduct our own lives. If we can follow this path more and more, we must—at the same time—allow, and even at times insist, on others doing likewise instead of continuing to rely on us to carry their responsibilities for them.

However, this route does not necessarily lead to our being popular in their eyes. Most people much prefer to persuade someone else to carry their responsibilities for them. But to allow them to be so dependent merely keeps them from having the opportunity to strengthen their own muscles by shouldering their own challenges instead of shirking them, or expecting someone else to undertake the fulfillment of them.

Public figures are more apt to be expected to assume this added burden, due, partly, to the myth that has been created that gives the impression they are bigger and more powerful and wise than they actually are.

I have observed that as I have become known by more people because of my work, many expect me to wave a magic wand to heal them of physical diseases, show them how to become wealthy, successfully solve their marital problems, miraculously change their children so that they behave as the parents think they should, and many other magical feats. I have learned through this work that even if I possessed such abilities I would refuse to use them in such a way, as it would only prevent, or at best, delay, each person's progress to have someone else go through the learning, testing, and training for them. Each one of us is responsible for working out our own individual karma. We cannot take over that job for someone else and no one else can be responsible for us.

CHAPTER 5

HOW DREAMS CAN
INDICATE PATCHES

For several years many people have been asking me to write a book on the method I have been taught to interpret dreams. But other books had to be written first. I don't decide the subject for each book from my own ego or desire any more than I decide ahead of time what I will be saying when I am asked to give a talk or conduct a seminar. I know only too well that I am not equipped either to talk or write from my limited personal knowledge, and to try to do so would only lead to failure and embarrassment. So, when I look back over the past few years, I am surprised to see that completely unknown to me, the books have followed a significant sequence.

For instance, when the concept of this book was first revealed, I had no inkling that it would incorporate a section on dreams. But it's not a whole book, which may come later. It's a case of, "Not when I decide, but in your time, Hi C." In other words, "Thy will, not mine."

Now I see clearly that dreams and their interpretation are an added means with which to let go of the layers or patches obscuring the light. What are these patches composed of that still have some life remaining in them from past lives? What must be done with them now that we have brought them over into the present life?

They are composed of all of our attachments to a wide variety of both tangible and intangible objects, people, customs, habits, and many other attachments. It would appear to be a logical solution to decide to let go of them all in one grand gesture of surrender. But that's not possible, for the simple reason that we are usually completely unconscious of a large majority of them. We must first become aware of the patches and then let go of them one at a time, when they have achieved their purpose of bringing to our attention those things we still need to learn.

All the habits, inclinations, attitudes, desires, and the many roles we play form the personality and physical body we now inhabit. Each one of us assumes many diverse roles during our lifetime, some having had their inception in infancy and early childhood and some having been brought over from former lives. It can often seem as if we are interred in a prison with apparently no escape possible. But this prison can be dismantled one brick at a time, as we begin to recognize and then release the various aspects. To do so, we need to observe our own behavior with particular attention to the way other people react to us.

In some patchwork quilts, patches cut from the same fabric are repeatedly interspersed between other pieces. The same is true in our lives. The most important lesson is repeated many times until we finally accept the learning it offers us. Consider one of the patches to be an indication of a lack of patience or lack of tolerance, another could be a lack of compassion that now needs to be developed.

The conditions into which we were born provide the necessary ingredients to allow us to learn the various lessons to balance the karma we have accumulated, and which these very conditions were designed to teach. So the patchwork quilt can be likened to the program we have brought with us to balance our karma. All our family members are also necessary teachers. In fact, we can all instruct one another. But we have not been taught this very important fact. So we don't realize that we all have been given a wonderful opportunity, if only we could stop resisting it and stop complaining long enough to ask what the various lessons presented to us are capable of teaching us! We must, therefore, ask ourselves what are our faults or weaknesses, and what are the habits or flaws that we would like to correct?

In this exercise toward self-awareness, our dreams can help us detect flaws of which we may be unaware. To help with this detective work, we can consciously ask to be given a dream that will alert us to these unconscious tendencies. Few people appear to be aware that they can ask for a dream to help them in this way. I can easily recall a time when I would have deemed such an attempt quite ridiculous. Most people think that dreams just happen and never stop to ask why, or inquire where they come from.

Some people protest that they never dream, but that's not true. Everyone dreams, but not everyone is able to recall them upon awakening, or even remember having dreamed. They seem to melt away like snowflakes in the sun as soon as we endeavor to catch hold of them. So we have to be willing to make a consistent effort to recall them as soon as we become conscious of having dreamed.

There are two quite simple methods you can use to record dreams. One is to keep available (on a nearby table or shelf) a notebook and pen so you can record the dream.

This must be done as soon as you awaken, when the dream is still clear in your mind. There is a very useful pen available now—it has a tiny light attached, which makes it much easier to write without awakening a sleeping partner. So there is no excuse for not committing the dream to paper to preserve it before it fades from memory!

The other method is to have a tape recorder conveniently placed so you can speak into it as soon as you awaken with a dream still clear in your mind. With this method, you will have to listen to the recording and write down the contents of the dream later. Taping dreams might get you more vivid detail if you are one of those people who has detailed and involved dreams.

Dreams can be of great assistance in providing a mirror in which are reflected various aspects of ourselves that we may be completely unaware of until these dreams bring this material to our attention. Therefore, a method is required to interpret the messages contained in the dreams so that the dreamer can benefit from this valuable input.

There are many methods available for deciphering the messages in dreams, all of which can be helpful. However, again, as with writing books or giving talks and seminars, I did not decide on a method. It was given to me, when I asked for instruction, from the Hi C. It is by no means the only method, or even the best one, but it has proven to be a very simple way to observe the hidden or unconscious parts of ourselves. ("Unconscious" means not having any knowledge or conscious awareness of something that other people might find obvious.) When people try to point out a habit or something of which we are unaware, our first quick reaction is often to assume, and even to tell them, that they are imagining it, or that it is untrue. For this reason, it is useless and a waste of time and energy to point out a very obvious fault, habit, or reaction to other people until they are ready to accept it. Otherwise, they will not believe what is being related to them and will discount it as being a figment of our imagination—an illusion.

Dreams originate from within each dreamer, so we are being shown things of which we were not previously aware, by a part of ourselves, not by someone else. Because it is our own insight, it can be more readily accepted. Then we will be able to release yet another block to self-awareness.

So just as the actual people in our lives can act as a mirror to reveal some of our own hidden tendencies, the people who appear in our dreams can be used in the same way.

In order to take advantage of the insights being given to us in dreams it is first essential to make a list of all the people who are known to us who appear in a dream as soon as possible upon awakening in the morning. The next step is to write down everything that comes to mind to describe each person. What is each one like as far as personality, traits, habits, attributes, faults, and so forth, are concerned? Is each one honest and trustworthy, caring and compassionate, lazy, habitually unpunctual, domineering, fearful, or a worrier?

In this way, each person can indicate an aspect of ourselves of which we may be unaware. By appearing in a dream they can alert us to the need to decide whether we should cut the ties to the negative qualities being brought to our attention. Or we may be lacking some positive aspects expressed by some of the people in a dream, in which case, we can concentrate on developing them.

Dreams can also bring to our attention the various roles we have assumed that are enacted by people in the dream, so that we can cut the ties to them and be free from constantly playing a role, even though it may be inappropriate in some circumstances.

If parents feature in a dream, we are probably being shown their attitudes around various subjects to which we have reacted during childhood and now need to be released from their continued control.

Obviously, it is absolutely essential to be completely honest and willing to recognize and accept things about ourselves that are being revealed by the dreams so that we can proceed to remove their control over us, for it has caused us to continue to act in a certain way that is no longer correct.

As can be seen, we need to be our own detective to decode the messages presented in our dreams before we can correct our mistakes. Try to remember that we cannot—and should not—even try to change other people. That is their responsibility and we would be stealing from them the opportunity to strengthen their own muscles if we were to try to do it for them. We can only succeed in bringing about changes in ourselves. Actually, that is a big enough undertaking for most people, but with our dreams to help us it is much easier to accomplish.

PART II
KARMIC
INDICATORS

CHAPTER 6

THE THEORY OF KARMA

THE THEORY OF KARMA and all that it entails is becoming more generally accepted, but for many people it still remains an unpopular concept. One of the chief reasons for resistance to this controversial subject is the common practice of preferring to cast the blame for our problems—and everything of an unpleasant nature that happens to us—onto someone or something other than ourselves, which is an utterly useless activity. We have been taught by the work with the Hi C that we attract to us exactly what we need to enable us to increase our understanding of who we are, and why we are here, and to develop such attributes as patience, tolerance, honesty, compassion, and other yin qualities to balance the over-development of yang (or aggressive and thought-controlled) tendencies that are so widespread in the world.

Instead of criticizing other people, we need to turn our attention to ourselves and take responsibility for our own growth and development, which is the reason we have incarnated again. Most of us would prefer to believe that we have always acted like angels in all our past lives, but I am sure that is far from the case! Having been given the opportunity to uncover some of my own former appearances on Earth, I can vouch for the fact that in some of them I behaved in ways that were anything but angelic.

I have been taught a theory that appears to me to be much closer to the truth. Karma can be compared to a boomerang or a homing pigeon, both of which are sent out into the world, but are bound to return to the one who sent them forth in the first place.

With every thought, feeling, word, and deed we use our own energy as the motor force to activate all these activities. In fact, we can accomplish absolutely nothing without the expenditure of our energy. So we project it out into manifestation clothed or contained in various forms according to the outcome we wish to achieve.

For instance, we might think or speak ill of someone with no awareness of the effect of our thoughts and words on the poor target of our criticism. But because we used our own energy to project these barbs to some hapless individual, they must return to us at some time in the future in the same form in which we launched them in the past, or possibly earlier in the present life, in which case it can be thought of as quick karma. The same theory applies to our acts, but with those, the results are more obvious, so it is easier to observe the cause and effect. But what we often fail to comprehend is that we ourselves, and not anyone else, initiated all of them, so they must return to us at some time that is conducive to our receiving them and learning from them.

Some people think it is essential to be regressed into their past lives to recall them in detail. In fact, it has become quite fashionable to engage in this type of investigation, but, it is not always necessary, or even advisable. To relive some past episodes could have an adverse effect by imprinting them more deeply on the subconscious instead of releasing them. It is usually sufficient to evaluate whatever we are undergoing in the present and inquire how we might have initiated each happening at some time in the past.

We forget that it is much more important for the subconscious part of the mind to receive the message that the "life" still left in the patch has now been used up, and we are free to concentrate on other patches that still contain energy that needs to be released, so it can be used more constructively. Only by accepting the lesson offered by each patch can we discard them. We can ask ourselves if we are ready to accept the lesson being presented to us with patience and a genuine desire to reverse an old negative attitude, or are we determined to reject it and complain bitterly and rail against our fate.

Do we find ourselves in a position in which we are required to carry an unusually heavy load of responsibility, which causes us to groan under the enforced burden, wondering what could possibly be the reason for this intolerable situation? Perhaps in a past life we avoided responsibility, and by escaping from accepting it as our duty, caused others to suffer by being forced to carry it for us.

Are we in a relationship now in which our partner, or other person close to us, is extremely selfish and egotistical? Maybe at some time we were equally self-involved and now need to experience how difficult such an attitude can be for all those with whom we come in close contact, whether in our family setting, in our workplace, or socially.

Were we unnecessarily harsh in a position of authority in which we meted out punishment to offenders for their crimes? What is happening in our present life to help us to become more aware of the painful effect of such behavior on our part? Did we choose to be born to parents who were inordinately strict? Were we responsible for stifling anyone's creativity, and are we suffering from being too restricted in some way now?

These examples are just a few suggestions to start us on our way to question what we might have done in the past that we are now being given an opportunity to equalize in the present. But we have to be our own detectives, and look very closely at our own situation with all the so-called problems and frustrations and ask ourselves, with a sincere desire to understand, what in our life is now available to help us to correct our former behavior and make amends for our past mistakes?

Everything that happens in life offers an opportunity to break away from attachment to someone or something that controls us other than the Hi C. So, the apparent traumas, when approached with this thought in mind, can show us the need to cut the ties to still more security objects or authority figures. As soon as we are aware of the opportunity to let go, and we stop trying to control the situation that was necessary to indicate it, it will disappear. If we refuse to accept it and try to resist or fight it, we will be adding to its power to affect us. Actually, if we can bring ourselves to thank the Hi C for the condition, situation, or relationship that is causing us suffering, we can hasten its departure.

Of course, it requires that we be willing to expend our time and effort to observe the many varied conditions, experiences, and relationships, and inquire what kind of behavior in the past is now being returned to us in the identical form. This kind of self-scrutiny is most rewarding if we are strictly honest and willing to face squarely the possible causes of our present problems. It does not necessarily remove all the difficult conditions overnight; it most certainly does allow us to understand and accept them and maybe even at some time be able to consider them as blessings.

In this context, I am reminded of a touching little story involving Sai Baba that was recounted to me by a witness. The parents of a young girl took her to see Baba, hoping that he would consent to heal her of a most disfiguring skin condition on both her arms. They were granted an interview, and when Baba asked them what they wanted, they fervently pleaded with him to heal their young daughter's arms. It is reported that Baba appeared to think for a second before answering their request. He then asked them if they were certain that they really wanted him to do what they were asking of him. Promptly and with intense emotion, they assured him that this was what they wanted. He then looked at them with great compassion and said that if he were to heal her now, she would have to return in another life with the same condition, and in that life she might not have such loving parents to care for her. He then asked them if they were still sure they wanted her to be healed. They regretfully replied, "No, not under those circumstances." It must be that this child had a particular patch carried over from a former life in which energy still remained, so at some time she would be forced to accept it as her heritage from past actions, for it still had life in it that had not yet been expended.

This episode answers the question posed by so many people of why some people are healed and others never seem to improve, no matter how many healing methods they may try.

It appears that there is no magic wand that can be waved to free everyone from their afflictions. Unless each person is willing to accept whatever conditions he or she attracted for his or her own good, and work to discard negative traits and replace them with positive ones, no healing will take place. I myself have sought far and wide for relief from some of the physical conditions from which I have suffered for most of my life. But, until I had used up the energy stored in the old negative actions and replaced them with positive ones, there was no surcease. I must admit that before I had been taught the reason for such continuous lack of success, I was extremely frustrated, and along with many others, asked, "Why me?" when I knew I had tried so hard in this life to cultivate positive traits.

I hope that by sharing this knowledge and insight many others who suffer without let-up may be helped with their very natural doubts and confusion, and begin to understand what needs to be done. Freedom can be gained only by being willing to eradicate the cause of the illness which lies in their past, instead of continuing to be depressed by each fresh lack of success in relieving the symptoms. The current symptoms will disappear, and the patch discarded, when the energy contained in it is used in a more positive way.

To end this chapter, the following quotations from Sathya Sai Baba's teachings sum up this concept very clearly.

> One meaning of Karma that is popularly accepted is that it is one's destiny or fate, the inescapable writing on the brow which has to work itself out. There is no escaping it. But people forget that it is not written by some other hand. It is written by one's own hand and the hand that wrote it can also wipe it off."[*]

> Do not blame fate or *simlikhitham*, writing on the head, for your condition. The *lithitham* has been done by you yourself.[†]

---

[*]From, *Sathya Sai Speaks*, vol. 3 (Prasanthi Niliyam, India: Sri Sathya Sai Books and Publications, 1963), p. 86.
[†]From *Sathya Sai Speaks*, vol. 2 (Prasanthi Niliyam, India: Sri Sathya Sai Books and Publications, 1961–1962), pp. 114–115.

CHAPTER 7

A PERSONAL EXAMPLE OF HOW KARMA WORKS

AN INCIDENT OCCURRED in my own experience that illustrates a possible direct connection between a past life and a seemingly unnecessary accident in this present one. I had returned to Hamburg, a city in Germany where my husband died of a massive heart attack during an earlier visit. While there, I was asked to give a talk when I attended a local Sai Baba center for their Thanksgiving celebration. We were asked to write down all the things that came to our minds for which we would like to thank Baba. The lists were collected and read aloud so that we could all benefit from the various suggestions.

I then gave a talk on this theme and ended it by saying that Baba wants us to be thankful for everything in our lives, whether we either like or dislike what we receive. All are gifts from which we can benefit in some way, even though we may not yet be ready or willing to agree.

After the talk, we made our way out of the hall down some steps leading to the parking area. Suddenly, and for no observable reason, I fell forward against and onto an iron railing, hitting my face and head, which caused my nose and mouth to bleed profusely. I was surrounded by devotees, as we were all leaving together, but no one was able to stop this accident. Even though I had foreseen it happening, I could not stop myself from falling. A friend who was at my side told me later that he was as if paralyzed, and could not move to help me either, much as he had tried. He rushed me to a hospital to have x-rays taken, and when we arrived, I realized to my horror, that it was the same hospital where my late husband had been taken five years earlier and where he died.

A doctor examined me, but it was too late to have an x-ray as the technician was not available until seven o'clock the following morning. The doctor wanted me to stay in the hospital overnight to be ready for the x-ray in the morning. But the very thought of sleeping in the same hospital where my husband died was more than I could face, so I decided not to stay that night but to return the following morning. When the results of the x-rays were examined the doctor was amazed. The impact had just missed my glasses, which have glass lenses as I am allergic to plastic ones, so I could have been blinded. In addition, I hit the iron railing just below the bones in my nose and cheeks, so none were broken, though my nose and gums were badly injured. If it had to happen, it was far less serious than it could have been, which Baba has promised will be the case if we call on him for help. He says he will not act contrary to our karma, but he will accelerate it and lessen the effect as much as possible. This, he most certainly did this time, for I was able to fly to Cologne the following day, where I had been asked to give a talk at the German yearly Sai Baba conference. I must have looked a mess, but I was able to deliver the talk without any problem, thanks to the Hi C's, or Baba's help.

"Why did it happen?" many people have asked. Obviously, I needed to experience it for some as yet unknown reason, probably originating in a past life of which I had, at that time, no recollection. However, when it happened, I did have a choice. I could bemoan my fate, or I could put into practice what I had just said to the devotees at the Sai center: accept it and give thanks for being given the opportunity to erase one more patch of karma.

Several weeks later, when the painful physical results of this accident had subsided somewhat, so I was no longer consciously aware of it, I had a sudden insight concerning its possible original cause. The memory of one of the past lives I had retrieved many years earlier came to my mind, and with it the realization that this recent accident could be a direct result of my action in that other life.

I had recalled with intense emotion a life as a Tibetan monk who had, at the direction of his teacher, agreed to allow himself to be closed in a cave for a certain length of time. The purpose of this interment was to make it possible for him to eliminate his desires, under the telepathic help of his teacher. However, the teacher was temporarily rendered unconscious, having been dropped while being carried on a platform by other monks in a procession during an important festival. That broke the telepathic connection between them. The immediate result of this cessation of the inner support from the teacher was so traumatic, and the desires from which he was endeavoring to detach himself became so overwhelming, that he banged his head against the wall of the cave in a helpless attempt to stop them from overpowering him. This desperate act caused him to bleed to death.

He initiated this action from his will and ego, and not from his Hi C, so he was actually attacking himself by an act of his own will, and in so doing, caused his own death, which we have been taught is the ultimate ego control. I was helpless to prevent the recent episode and was obliged to suffer the effects of that previous willful act.

Interestingly enough, on our first visit to Baba early in 1973, when Baba asked my husband what he wanted to be given, he replied that he would like my headaches to be cured. Baba then told me that I had five different kinds of headache, not just one, as I had thought. He assured me that he would help when I must have looked aghast at this news of five instead of one. He then proceeded to produce one of the "cures." He materialized a ring made from a combination of seven different metals, called Panchaloha. Set into the metal was a moonstone, which he directed me to rub on the center of my forehead every day, to heal one of the headaches, which I have done ever since. As Baba was explaining to me what I should do, my mind flew back to the Tibetan life which I had uncovered many years earlier, so I gasped, "Oh Baba," in amazement, to which he replied, "Yes, Swami knows all about your past, too." So, presumably, Baba helped me to remove the original cause, but still some vestiges of the old patch remained, which the strange accident may have finally removed.

I can only hope that in this way another patch has been unraveled from my patchwork quilt and will not have to be repeated.

CHAPTER 8

HOW PATCHES HELP US REMOVE KARMA

EACH PATCH ACTS LIKE a magnet that draws to each of us whatever is needed for our learning. This includes the people in our life, as well as the illnesses, events, experiences, and everything with which we will be faced in this lifetime. Not all the patches can be de-energized in one life. It depends on the attitude of each of us and whether we are willing to accept the various circumstances, or inquire what each one can teach us. We all have a certain amount of free will as far as our attitude is concerned. We can, for instance, accept the many varied experiences, or we can resist them, and refuse to learn from them, preferring to complain and rail against fate, or God, or the Universe. But as Sathya Sai Baba tells us, the hand that wrote the script for each life is the hand that must erase it. So it is up to each one of us to make up our minds to start asking what each event can teach us, and stop blaming other people or outer authorities, for we alone are responsible for everything that occurs in our life.

This is an extremely hard lesson for most people. We all find it so much easier to cast the blame outside ourselves than to recognize this fact and accept and deal with whatever happens. In order to do so, we must ask what we still need to learn that we failed to learn in previous lives. Then we can watch to see which people or events will supply the means by which we can develop more positive qualities. As we start to recognize that our so-called problems are actually opportunities, we will find the patches will fall away. At such time when all are removed or emptied of energy, the light we really are, and always have been, will become visible and we will be able to express the love from our Real Self to all those who appear on our path.

I was recently informed that Yogananda is reputed to have said that many souls would seek incarnation in the latter part of the 20th century because they would have the opportunity to work out the karma from several lives instead of from only one. This message makes it easier to understand why so many of us are having to face, accept, and deal with many very severe problems, whether they are physical, mental, emotional, or spiritual.

This is possibly one of the reasons why Sathya Sai Baba has taken human birth at this time in history, as apparently has been the case in the past when other avatars and great teachers have inhabited Earth at times of great crisis, such as the present.

Instead of allowing the events in our lives to depress us so that we give up and suffer, but do nothing to help the situation, we can ask the Hi C for the strength to deal with each fresh problem. Only when we ask with the conviction that we will receive help shall we find that we have been given the strength and wisdom to solve each problem. If we merely collapse, enveloped in self-pity, we will make no progress, and will continue to suffer unnecessarily, and eventually become paralyzed and unable to help ourselves. A radical change of attitude is required, one that is in direct opposition to everything we have been taught. "Why me?" or "Poor little me," have to be discarded and replaced with, "What can this teach me?" or "How can I overcome or solve this problem with the help of the Hi C?" Such a change of attitude will prevent us from sinking into depression and helplessness, for they are conditions that prevent us from solving anything.

This practice can be looked upon as a kind of treasure hunt in which certain clues are given to us. By following these clues or signs we can find the treasure, which is release from the effects of our past deeds. That allows us to discard some of the patches we brought over with us from the past. Looked at in this way, life can be an adventure, for we never know which patch is being worked out next.

Since each patch is brought over from a past life when the soul inhabited a different body/personality sheath, the combination of these patches from many prior lives forms a new body/personality or patchwork quilt. In this way we are given an opportunity to expend the remaining energy in each patch by learning the particular lesson that had not been completed at an earlier time. When the remaining life or energy in each patch is used up, it falls away like an old skin, or a worn-out piece of cloth, until so few patches remain that the light of the Hi C that was once obscured is now fully exposed. As can be surmised, this process can extend over many lifetimes, for in each life new patches are formed and many of the old ones may still be very much alive.

To many people, this theory is intimidating. They feel overwhelmed by the seemingly enormous task confronting them and helplessly give up any attempt to undertake it. But life has a habit of presenting us with situations that are exactly what we need to enable us to discard at least a few patches in each lifetime. Yet this unconscious approach is very slow and could take many lifetimes to complete.

In this present Kali Yuga, the very aspects that make it appear so negative are actually those conditions that exert so much pressure on us that we are forced to accelerate our growth and learning or be defeated. Fortunately, many methods are emerging to help those who are willing to make a conscious effort to remove some of the old patches by means of self-observation. This way leads to understanding and learning what was not learned in previous lives.

In order for the Real Self or Hi C to be revealed, all the overlay (which is like a lampshade) needs to be removed so the light can shine forth in its full splendor. The result is known as illumination, enlightenment, or Self-Realization. The light, or Hi C, can then operate in each person's life instead of the ego being in control.

One method that can assist in such an operation is the one that has been gradually revealed to me over a span of many years. It is not the only method. It is, however, effective in enabling those who are willing to use it regularly to remove the patches one at a time. Whether this practice will eventually lead to enlightenment is not as important as the learning derived from engaging in it. It is not the goal but the process that requires our full attention, for when sincerely undertaken, it can lead us step-by-step to the goal of union with the Hi C, for we cannot achieve the goal directly and without effort, or in one huge leap.

Cutting the Ties That Bind can free those who are willing to use it from many of the patches that have been inherited from past behavior. By removing these patches that form the overlay that obscures the Real Self, It will obviously be increasingly revealed and given Its rightful place in our lives as the only reliable director. If we look closely at each of the patches that compose the covering over our light, we can really let that light shine.

There are many ways to catch glimpses of these innumerable, but frequently unconscious overlays we have accumulated over our many lifetimes. They force us to continue to return into yet more births until we are finally free to be who we are and who we always have been, even though we were previously unaware of our true identity.

The ever-increasing stress that is experienced by the majority of people in their daily lives can well be the very means to compel them to break through their lethargy and be free. Each new life gives us that opportunity. This present life could spur us forward out of sheer frustration at our own shortcomings and problems. In this way we start to view all our problems as the actual means by which to overcome the frustration and stress.

A mantra that was introduced to me in meditation provides a formula for success in this endeavor. It is, "Surrender, Trust, and Accept." We can make a conscious decision to *surrender* our personal will to that of the Hi C. It is far superior to our own limited personality, so we can *trust* It to provide us with precisely what we need for our evolution. Then we have to *accept* whatever is forthcoming. This practice will initiate the return to our Source from which we have been separated for too long. As soon as we start to rely on It to guide us and allow It to live through us, It will open up many unforseen opportunities that will eventually lead us out of the darkness created by our ego and into the light of our true essence.

However, there is the danger that we may have such a strong desire for enlightenment that, instead of letting go of all the impediments, we will attempt to give the impression of being enlightened, while still acting according to the dictates of the ego. Such people wear their assumed spirituality as a badge or a veneer. But it is of no avail to try to apply the light from outside or wear it as a role or mask. That will only act as an additional lampshade or patchwork quilt of old patterns beneath which the real light is still hidden.

We are largely unconscious of who we are. We have been taught since childhood to consider the body, mind, and personality as the real person. We must use a mirror to see all the outer patches that have to be released to reveal the Hi C. One of the best ways to catch sight of the overlay is with the help of dreams.

Chapter 9

How to Deactivate the Patches

WE HAVE NOW SEEN how we bring into each new life a patchwork quilt composed of various aspects from former lives that still have "life" in them, and which can show us what we still have to learn. We must first become conscious of them before we can release them. In so doing, we allow the Hi C the freedom to be our only guide.

This is not a pleasant task. None of us enjoys addressing our faults. Most of us prefer to hide them. We ignore their very existence and pretend to ourselves—as well as to others—that we are as pure as driven snow! So what are these blemishes on our character that we prefer not to confront? They are different for each of us, depending on the patches we have, at the Hi C level, agreed to work on in this life.

A few common blemishes are: anger, jealousy, envy, greed, avarice, pride, vanity, fear, control, aggression, egoism, selfishness, sloth, laziness, and many more. If looked at carefully, it becomes evident that they are all attached or caused by various desires. We either want something or someone, or try to avoid something we do not want.

However, we should not even think of attempting to deal with them all at once. That would be far too daunting a task to undertake and would most probably result in our postponing it indefinitely, or until such time in the future when we think we might be better able to face it. A helpful method in uncovering and discarding these unattractive aspects involves using a package of multicolored postcards or note paper on which to record them.

Choose a card of a specific color on which to record instances when you catch yourself expressing each negative emotion. Envy could be listed on a green card, as in "green with envy," jealousy on a yellow card with which it is usually associated, white for fear since many people turn white or lose their color when they register fear, anger on red as it often causes the blood to rush into an angry person's face, so that it is flushed, and so forth.

It is best to work with only one of these emotions at a time to avoid being overwhelmed by too much to do, which can deter you from making a start. Each of you will have brought different emotions to work on, in which case you can add your own and proceed in a similar way to the method previously outlined for each negative emotion that follows.

By watching the people who frequent your dreams, some of the patches of which you may be unconscious will be brought to your attention. Everyone who appears in a dream bears a message for the dreamer, since each one can be used as a mirror in which to catch sight of one of our patches. So, if you dream of someone who is angry, jealous, envious, or has any of the other negative traits, then look for the same reaction in yourself, with the understanding that you may be literally unconscious of such behavior in yourself until the dream draws it to your attention in this way.

CHAPTER 10

PAST CONTROL AND ITS PRESENT EFFECT

W̲ʜᴇɴ ᴡᴇ ᴀʀᴇ ᴄᴏɴᴛʀᴏʟ-
ling toward others, we frequently have not the slightest
awareness that they may be extremely sensitive to our behavior. So what better way to learn that lesson than by
being born in a later life as a super-sensitive person? In the
present life it would be appropriate to be more than normally sensitive in order to become fully aware of just how
painful it can be to be treated in an insensitive way.

Sensitivity includes reacting not only to controlling people, but to any and all strong and abrasive conditions, such
as loud noises, extremes of heat and cold, strong perfumes,
hot spicy food, strong light, and a host of other irritants that
other people barely notice. Instead of bemoaning our fate,
if we happen to belong in this category, we would do better
to ask why we came into this life in such a sensitive body.
Could it be that we need to be more compassionate of others who are also sensitive? The only way we can learn is by
experiencing the very conditions in our present life that we
caused others at a previous time. If we have acted in an in-

sensitive way to others, we can understand how painful our behavior was only by having to suffer at the hands of insensitive people ourselves. I repeat, "The hand that wrote the script is the hand that must erase it." Only in this way can we comprehend that our former behavior was wrong, and once we are able to accept this fact we can remedy it. By doing so the energy still contained in one of the patches is used up and the worn-out patch can be discarded.

Many illnesses and afflictions can be accounted for in this way. So, the sooner we ask ourselves, "What could I have done in a past life to attract this condition to me in this present one?" the faster we can be free of the patch.

Many people are appalled at such a concept, and argue that they have been unselfish and loving throughout this life, so why should they be faced with so many problems? I repeat, we would all prefer to believe that we have been angels in the past, but this is definitely not the case. It has taken many lifetimes of learning, as well as many in which we have failed to learn the necessary lessons, continuing along a very selfish and negative path. So it is not only how we have acted in this life that determines what happens to us, but how we have acted in the past. If we have caused harm to anyone, whether by thought, feeling, word, or deed, we must expect to receive the same cruel treatment ourselves to balance the scales of justice. This belief cuts out any reason to blame other people, fate, or the world situation. These outer forces merely provide the occasion and circumstances for us to receive what we ourselves gave out at a previous time. We alone are responsible, not anyone or anything else.

So, we draw to ourselves the present body with whatever we need to inherit from both our mother's and father's family line. I am often amazed when meeting several children from the same two parents, each of whom have inherited different characteristics from the family stockpile of collective genes. Some of the siblings inherit a tendency that results in a physical condition, while others inherit a mental or emotional problem, depending on what part of their karma they have, at the Hi C level, undertaken to work out in this life.

I remember when this interesting and challenging concept was first introduced in the work. It was such a profound relief for me to know that I was not directly responsible for the fact that both my daughters had inherited various problems from my family heritage. From my husband's side of the family they had taken different conditions.

Many people find that an astrological chart is helpful in indicating various inherited tendencies in a newborn infant. I did not value astrology at one point, for it seemed to be too illogical. This appeared to be particularly true in the case of babies who were born by means of Caesarean section, for the doctor or parents generally determine the date of the birth. The same appeared to be the case where, for some reason, the labor of the mother was artificially induced. However, I have had to change my mind after having seen some babies' charts that I have ordered and given as gifts to the parents. Not only have I been amazed by what was indicated about the many different aspects of the baby, but the parents have also been extremely grateful for the help a chart gives them in rearing the child.

The next question is, "Why did we inherit particular traits?" The only reason I have been able to accept is that the Hi C knows what each one of us still needs to undergo in order to learn whatever we failed to learn until now, and provides the means for us to do so.

In India, for centuries, astrology has been accepted as a way to indicate a person's heritage. In addition, it is used as a guide for choosing a marriage partner. In that case, the charts of both the man and woman considering marriage are consulted to determine whether they will be compatible. In the East many marriages are arranged by both sets of parents with the help of an astrologer, instead of by two young people choosing to marry, as is the custom in the West. I used to look with disfavor at arranged marriages, but having observed some of these unions, and comparing them with those I have observed in the West, I am inclined to believe that the arranged marriages may, in some cases, be more successful. This may be because they are founded on common backgrounds and character traits rather than the often haphazard reasons, such as sexual attraction, that we are more accustomed to seeing in the West.

Given the fact that we inherit whatever we need for our growth, it is a comfort to bear in mind that as soon as we have worked out in the present life whatever was left unfinished before, we will no longer need the condition that helped us to do so.

At this time, when we are all being offered an opportunity to clear away more of the old patches, many different therapies and healing methods are being initiated to help us release some of the old worn-out patterns of behavior. Cutting the ties that bind us to anyone or anything that controls us is one such method. Many healers are also making themselves known and are being accepted and sought by many who find conventional methods to be ineffective for healing certain problems. Some of these new methods are helping people discard old conditions that are no longer useful. But, as usual, with any method, if the karma has not yet been balanced, the condition will not improve.

I myself, have, through the years, sought out a number of unorthodox methods in the hope of removing the various health problems I have had. But at the same time, I have tried to determine the reason for these conditions, and have asked how I can equalize them.

Sai Baba says that selfless service is the best way to offset old negative karma. By helping others with their problems, we are indirectly healing ourselves. But those who expect other people to wave a magic wand empowered to dispel their problems are missing the whole point of this life. We can only change ourselves. No one can do that for us, nor can we accomplish it for anyone else. It requires dedication, perseverance, and determination. We cannot expect to be saved by someone else.

Other people can be of great help, but only if we are also willing to do our part by living in the present without negative thoughts, feelings, words, or actions toward anyone. I have found that the best way to remain aware of this requirement is by means of a daily ritual. It consists of asking the Hi C first of all to *think* through me all day, since we can do nothing unless we have first thought of what we will do. Next, I ask the Hi C to *feel* through me all day. This is necessary in order to energize the thought, for without the desire or emotion, thoughts can remain arid and sterile. We have all heard of "head trips" that never develop beyond the mind, that live as fantasies or daydreams. After thought and emotion are linked, we must put whatever we plan to do into words, so I ask the Hi C to *speak* through me all day. Only after taking these steps can we get anything accomplished, so then I ask the Hi C to *act* through me all day. I usually count these steps on the fingers of one hand. One finger is still left. With this one I ask the Hi C to *love* through me all day, for without love all the other steps will be hollow. But with love, they will be energized by the Hi C. (TFSAL is one way to remember it!)

With this simple little exercise, we are assured that we will incur no further karma, as the Hi C will be the doer, instead of the ego, as in the past. This activity can bring about release and eventual freedom from karma.

Some of us have ventured forth onto an inner path in a prior life, but along the way the ego had taken over and convinced us that we are the doer and not the Hi C. When this happens, control takes over and we will seek many ways to control others, and will also try to control our own fate. This can be likened to a fall from grace, which will need to be remedied at some future time when circumstances permit, and we have learned that we are not the body, mind, or ego, but the Hi C.

This life has given me a chance to start again on the inner path, but this time, remain ever wary of the temptation to allow the ego to take over instead of having the Real Self or Hi C be the guide. In order to accomplish this task, I was born into an extremely sensitive body and had many allergies. Baba once informed me that in this life my karma would be worked out in my body, and that my body could be likened to the Kurukshetra, the battlefield where the war between the forces of good and evil was waged, as recorded in the epic Bhagavad Gita. I interpreted this statement to mean that I was working out what I had put into action at a previous time on the physical level. So this time I have been afflicted with physical problems to which there have never appeared to be any solutions. I used to wonder why other people would be relieved of their illnesses by various healing methods, but I still continued to be beset by mine. I investigated a number of methods, but never did they do for me what they apparently did for other people. Obviously, I had not sufficiently erased the karma which my Hi C had elected to have me take over in this life.

I have often heard myself comment that when my car needs fixing I can leave it in a garage where a mechanic will work on it, and it will be returned to me in good condition. But, I have often lamented that we are not able to do that with our bodies! The only way we can reverse some of the negative health problems is to learn whatever lesson they are here to teach us. Then, in many instances, the condition will disappear.

As I was writing this section of the book, I was undergoing a series of interesting treatments in England. Each day I went to a healer who performed various psychic operations, in addition to the laying on of hands. He said that he doesn't personally do any healing, but that he is the instrument through whom unseen helpers heal the many sick people who seek his help. He is a sincere devotee of Sai Baba, and says that Baba often heals through him, and "appears" to some clairvoyant patients, even to those who have never heard of him.

As I was attending these healing sessions, I felt like the car that had been taken to the mechanic, as my treatments, which ranged from "operations," to laying on of hands, to applications of vibhuti, and sips of lingam water, were changing my body. I most sincerely hope that I have erased enough of the old karma by sharing the Hi C method I have been taught. Maybe I can now be free from some of the physical disabilities I have experienced. I hope my story gives you courage to continue on through your own growth.

CHAPTER 11

THE PEOPLE IN OUR LIVES

I REMEMBER MY FIRST reaction when I was presented with the possibility that my family members and close relationships were chosen to help me to balance my karma, as I in turn gave them the same chance to work out some of theirs. "Could this also apply to my mother?" I queried in dismay and disbelief. Could my Hi C have chosen her precisely to allow me to remove some of the patches? My next question was, "Have I used this relationship in the way it was designed to teach me?" I had to admit that I had not even been aware of the opportunity it offered me, let alone benefit from it. But now, as I look back from this present vantage point, I can clearly observe that she was one of my best teachers, though I certainly did not believe that while I was growing up under her extremely harsh treatment.

Sai Baba assures us that those people with whom we spend the most time, such as close family members, are the very ones who can best enable us to face those facets of ourselves that we still must explore.

My mother was extremely controlling, but I have learned that in the past, I too, controlled many others, and now needed to live under similar control in order to understand how it felt, and how wrong it was to attempt to control others as I had done. Apparently, I had not fully used this relationship with my mother to learn this lesson, so I needed to continue with the help of a husband who was also very controlling. Sai Baba once told me in the presence of my husband that this present life with him was much more helpful for my spiritual growth than an entire life as a sadhak (or renunciate), for it could teach me patience, tolerance, steadfastness, and forbearance.

This statement set me to thinking. I quickly realized that these qualities were sadly lacking in my makeup. I knew that I had always been impatient and reacted too quickly. Also, when I was in college in England, I was told I was an intellectual snob, and that I was impatient and intolerant of those who were, in my opinion, too slow. What better way to teach me than by being born to a mother who punished me severely, but never told me the reason, and when I asked what I had done to deserve the punishment, beat me for being impertinent and for questioning her authority! I never knew if I had done something wrong, or if I had left undone something I should have done. This treatment resulted in extreme insecurity. However, I have learned through my work that those born into a family where they found no security in the parents or other family members are the very ones who are destined to take the inner path to find their security in the Hi C rather than in outer authority or security in people or objects.

This requires steadfastness to accomplish instead of giving up when life appears to be too difficult. Forbearance was also something I had to learn. It is the ability to restrain oneself from hitting back or retaliating when someone causes pain or embarrassment. Here again, the temptation to do so as a child was not practical, for I knew I would have incurred even more punishment had I attempted it. I see now that only in this way could I have learned how frustrating it is to be under another person's control. The result of such a childhood was a determination never to do to others what I had been forced to endure.

However, we are all striving to achieve balance, even when we are not conscious of that fact. We need to beware of overreacting, or becoming too much of a door mat and allowing others to determine our destiny. There is a very fine line between these two extremes. Eventually, we all need to cut the ties with all outer authority and security figures, or objects, so we can more easily and directly seek the guidance of the Hi C.

When I finally learned through my work to cut the ties with my mother, and went through that ritual, she did not change, neither did she have any idea of what I had done. However, on a deep level she must have sensed the change, and resented the fact that I was no longer under her control. But I was free from reacting to her, and could rely on my inner voice to direct me instead of obeying her constant demands.

This all sounds deceptively simple, but it is actually a slow step-by-step process that needs to be practiced daily until you are secure in your inner guidance. You'll know when you have made an important cut, because you will feel the change inside you.

Obviously, what I needed was to have my strong will and the need to be in control reduced in this life. My mother used to boast (when I was a child) that she had broken my will. Such was not quite the case. She had succeeded in forcing me to withdraw and live within in my own world. So I apparently became very obedient and docile to all outer appearances, and sought security in my dreams and fantasies. I was neither seen nor heard, which made it possible to cope with my mother's demands, but caused me to be painfully shy and withdrawn, fearing that others would try to control me as my mother did, and preferring to become as invisible as possible to avoid her angry attacks.

But what better way to teach me how a former very controlling life must have affected the people I had so thoughtlessly controlled? This was a rather big patch brought over from the far distant past, and one I hope I am succeeding in draining of its energy and life on many different levels.

Many people find that when they ask the Hi C to indicate the person from whom they should cut the ties, sometimes two people may appear. Usually they are a parent and a partner.

As I have mentioned before, if the karmic debt is a heavy one, it is often necessary to repeat the lesson that began with one of the parents by continuing with a partner, who invariably is similar to the parent. In that case, the Hi C needs to be consulted in order to discover which of the two people should be worked on first. I hear from so many people the lament, "I married my mother," or, "I married my father."

It has been indicated in the work that groups of souls often incarnate at the same time to help one another work out the karma from their various patches. Sometimes the relationship between them can create confusing situations if the former one was so strong that it carries over into the present life. For example, if two people in a past life were husband and wife, and in their present life they are now mother and son, father and daughter, or some other close relationship, there is the possibility that the former role will overshadow the present one and create very difficult situations. In such cases, it is of the utmost importance to cut the ties with the past relationship and accept full responsibility for the current one, with its very different demands and patterns. These are all roles that we assume for the purpose of balancing our karma and correcting our behavior in the present so we will not create any new karma that will have to be worked out in a future life.

There are very specific guidelines that govern each of the roles associated with family relationships. We should follow these guidelines and not allow past roles to overshadow or prevent us from assuming the present ones.

We often see parents acting toward their children more as if they were wedded, instead of as parent and child. This is, of course, highly inappropriate, and causes severe problems for each person who is thus locked into the past in such a way that neither can assume the present role and live it out effectively. Many cases of incest stem from this tendency to repeat the past, instead of accepting the present relationship and learning what it is able to teach. These are all some of the patches we bring in with us to work out in the present.

It becomes clear that many of the relationships that cause us the most distress can, if looked at from this very different point of view, actually be the most helpful, by offering us the opportunity to divest ourselves of some of our patches. If someone appears to be unnecessarily antagonistic or critical, we can assume that we have, at some time in the past, acted in much the same way, and are now being given a ''taste'' of how our former behavior affected others. In this way, we can determine not to repeat the old patterns. Instead, we are now in a position to use the present relationship to observe in ourselves attitudes and habits that still need to be addressed.

I was recently informed of a study conducted to ascertain the affect of a father on his two sons. The father was imprisoned on many charges, including murder. Each of the sons was asked what effect their father's record had on his life. One of the sons was also in prison, though on lesser charges than those of his father. When asked this key question, he answered, "With such a father as an example, how could I have been any different?" His brother owned a successful business, was married, and had several children. When he was asked the same question, his answer was, "With such a bad example set by my father, how could I not have acted differently? He was provided as a warning to me not to follow in his footsteps."

We all have freedom to determine whether we will mimic the behavior of our parents, or take advantage of our birthright as human beings and decide to grow in the opposite direction when we are shown the results of their negative behavior.

In the above case, the father unknowingly was a teacher to both of his sons. One blindly followed in his father's footsteps, while the other son chose to be warned by the example set by his father, and decided to become responsible for his own life. Stories similar to this are also found in the Bible.

Apparently we have a certain amount of free choice as far as our acceptance of the events in our lives is concerned. If we use that gift wisely we will be able to avoid a great deal of the suffering that results from our unthinking reactions, or hasty decisions and actions.

There is no law that dictates that it is necessary to copy negative characteristics we have seen in our parents or others, just because we were exposed to negative examples of close family members while we were young and impressionable. Each one of us is responsible for the way we live, despite what we have been taught to the contrary. Eventually we will be forced by circumstances to understand that there is nobody in the whole world who either can, or has the right to tell us what to do or what not to do. Only we, ourselves, can make that decision, so it is best to start right now and waste no more time.

As we are willing to learn this very important lesson, we will automatically use up the energy in some of the patches we have brought with us for our progress.

CHAPTER 12

LEARNING WHEN TO SAY "NO"

BABA SAYS THAT WE cannot always oblige, but we should always speak and act obligingly. This, however, involves the willingness to say "No" to someone, if that person is insisting on our doing something that we feel strongly that we should not or cannot do. But saying "No" for some people is extremely difficult. For instance, we may be endangering our relationship with the person who is expecting us to do something. In that case, we may incur criticism and gossip which could throw a shadow on our own reputation. It could also result in actually disappointing some people by causing them to feel rejected, unloved, or in some way, inferior or unworthy. That is obviously why Baba cautions us to speak and act obligingly when we cannot go along with someone's request or demands.

I have noticed that when I must say "No," if I hesitate or waver, become defensive, angry, or apologetic, I have already lost my position, and the demanding person will swiftly seize the opportunity to move in even more strongly with a demand. However, if I remain centered and strong in my own conviction regarding what I should do, and state my position firmly, but in an even tone, without anger or nervousness, invariably the person will be agreeable and will not continue to pursue his or her demands. But even with these precautions, the person may still react with hurt feelings and disappointment, or may have to face a difficult situation without our intervention. In such a case, we must resist the temptation to give in to feelings of guilt, which can often be used by others as a ruse to achieve their desired effect.

It takes a tremendous amount of courage and strength to hold out against persuasion, accusations, criticism, or self-pity on the part of another person or group. Saying "No" is even more of a problem if there is a close relationship, particularly if it involves a partner or family member who knows exactly how to play on our weaknesses. We have to learn to be Spiritual Warriors and remain strong when facing opposition, no matter what the outcome will be, or how maligned we will be for our refusal to oblige, when to do so is in opposition to what we know to be correct action on our part.

I have recently had three experiences where I have had to say "No," and in doing so, I have disappointed many people. It has been extremely hard because I had a very controlling mother who insisted that I do everything she demanded of me, even if it was out of character for me to acquiesce. When I had to disagree with her demands, I would become the butt of her anger, so I dreaded the times when I could not agree implicitly with her. As long as I went along with her every whim, all was fairly peaceful. Otherwise it was very difficult. Because of this early programming, I found it to be almost impossible not to defer to the demands of others for fear of the consequences if I declined. So life situations had to force me to be discriminating and to recognize when to acquiesce and when to refuse. This lesson has had to be learned in both personal and group relationships. Refusing is not only correct when the request is in conflict with our own deep sense of what is right or wrong; sometimes a refusal is merely a matter of right timing.

I have also observed that by saying "No," the person receiving this answer will be given an opportunity to learn a lesson that he or she needs. In that case, if we accede to their wishes, we may be depriving them of this chance to change. We cannot always know the affect on others, so we must make sure to do whatever we feel is correct for us and let go of the result, as well as the affect the refusal may have on the person asking.

The three experiences that taught me this very much needed lesson were very hard to take. I had been asked to go to Belgrade in what is now Serbia, but was formerly Yugoslavia, to give seminars on my work. I made all the preparations to go for a weekend immediately following a visit to Croatia. I was driven to the airport in Trieste by my Croatian contacts to take the flight to Belgrade. When I arrived at the airport, I was asked for my visa. Since no one had informed me that I needed a visa, I did not have one, so I was not allowed to board the plane. What a dilemma! We called the organizer of the seminar and explained the problem. She said she would try to contact the office in Belgrade and see if they would grant me a visa and fax it to the airport in Trieste. However, she called back to report that the office was closed so there was nothing else we could do except to cancel the seminar, as the next flight, several days later, would arrive too late. It was very hard for me to be obliged to cancel the weekend at such short notice. I was fully aware of the disappointment of all the people who had already enrolled, and I felt badly for the organizer, who would have the difficult task of calling each one and explaining the situation, and who would probably be exposed to the anger of some of the disappointed participants. In this case, the decision was out of my hands, so I could do nothing to remedy it.

I was invited to Belgrade a second time and made sure that I had the necessary visa. So, armed with it, I was ready to go there in the middle of my next trip to Europe. But meanwhile, a situation had arisen in Serbia that resulted in the U. S. State Department issuing a warning to all Americans that it was not safe for them to travel in that country at that time. That was quite a shock. What should I do this time? Should I act against this advice and go anyway, or must I, once again, disappoint all the people who were expecting me? This time the decision had not been made for me as it had on the previous occasion. Now I was faced with the decision either to obey the warning and once more cancel the visit, or flout authority and go anyway. I was torn between prudence and my intense dislike of causing disappointment, and possibly a sense of rejection to those who were expecting me to appear. When I consulted the Hi C, the answer I received was quite clear that I must abide by the warning given by the government of my country as the situation had political ramifications.

As soon as I had made the decision, an interesting thing happened that reassured me that I had decided correctly. I was in the middle of giving a seminar at a location outside of Munich, Germany, when an officer of the Sai Organization drove out to bring me an invitation from the organizers of the yearly national Sai conference to be held in

Cologne. Apparently, they had just heard that I was in Germany, and wanted to know if I would be willing to be one of the speakers at the conference. Obviously, this invitation was my reassurance that Cologne was where I was supposed to be that weekend. I do not know the reason for this last-minute change of plans, only that I was clearly shown where I belonged. But again, I was genuinely disturbed to have to disappoint the people who had signed up for the seminar in Belgrade, especially as they were already under such stress from the political situation under which they lived. Actually, that was one of the reasons why they had asked me to visit, so that I could share with them some of the exercises I had learned in my work. The organizers, too, were very upset and I realized that it would appear that I was not dependable, so my reputation would also be questioned.

The third time I canceled an appointment it was even more difficult to make the decision. I had been invited to give a lecture and workshop at a conference in Northern California, designed to bring together speakers from the spiritual community with those involved in various psychological methods. I had agreed to participate, as it sounded like such an interesting combination, and could build a bridge between the two often opposing groups. Quite a time after I had promised to attend, I was at Sai Baba's ashram in India with my granddaughter, Crystal. At the end of our second interview, I found myself asking a question that I had no intention of asking Baba. It was, "When should I return?" Up until that moment I had concluded that my next visit would be when I was ready to take the manuscript of this book for his blessing, as I have done with each of the previous books. His answer came as a great surprise. He stepped close to my face and very slowly and deliberately said, "Youu-u come back in November," stressing the You and prolonging it for several seconds. Since November usually means his birthday to most devotees, as it falls on November 23rd, I immediately asked, "For your birthday, Swami?" to which he replied with an odd smile, "Very happy." It was not until I returned to my room that I remembered that I had agreed to attend the conference in Northern California, which was to take place from November 19th to the 22nd, leaving insufficient time to arrive at the ashram in time for the birthday. What was I to do? I discussed the situation with the organizer who offered to replace me if I wished. I was fully aware that Baba disapproves of breaking a promise once it has been given. So I asked the organizer if I could give the lecture and the workshop as early in the conference as possible, so that I could leave for India immediately following my presentation. He graciously agreed to this plan. That meant that I could not be present for Baba's birthday, as I would arrive several days later. But since Baba himself had said November and it was I who mentioned his birthday, I hoped this was what he had intended. So I made all the reservations for the two trips and had the tickets in hand months before I was due to leave.

Then, a few days before the conference I was informed that not many people had signed up to attend, so, remembering my plans to go to India, the organizer inquired if I would like to withdraw. My first reaction was to decline, since I had made the commitment. However, I was haunted by a strange feeling that I could not shake, that I should reconsider. First I called my travel agent to find out if I could still arrive for the birthday if I canceled my attendance at the conference. To my immense surprise, she informed me that I could fly straight through with only one slight glitch. I would have to change planes in Bangkok and fly to Bombay on a different carrier, but it would still allow me to arrive at the ashram around noon on the day of the birthday. I had very little expectation that there would be available seats at such short notice, especially at a festival time when so many people like to travel to the ashram. When I called the travel agent back to tell her to go ahead and book the flights, she informed me that since we had first spoken, a seat had become available from Bangkok on the same carrier, so I would not have to change planes, but could fly straight through. Was this the sign I was waiting for to help me to make the decision?

This time there was no definite outer indication to help me know what I should do. It rested entirely on my shoulders. Again, it would mean breaking a commitment as well as disappointing the people who had elected to attend my presentation at the conference. This was indeed a dilemma, and there was nothing to help me make the right decision. Then I recalled an occasion at the ashram when several of the officers of the U.S. organization were unexpectedly there at the same time. A problem had arisen in the California area involving a member of the council who had an extremely strong will and who was attempting to overrule the other members. So, a meeting was called for those members who were at the ashram at that time. My late husband was a member then, but I was not, as it was a rule to have only one member of a family on the council at the same time. The wives were allowed to attend meetings as long as they did not speak.

During the meeting, Baba would enter and stay for short periods and would listen to the discussions. When it came time to review the problem with the strong-willed member, Baba sat down to observe. As the discussion proceeded, a question arose in my mind, "How can we tell the difference between our own will, another person's will, and Baba's, so that we can take action only according to Baba's will! I did not, of course, voice my question, but since Baba is able to read our thoughts, he smiled as he said, "You have a question, Mrs. Krystal?" I replied, "I am not allowed to speak, as I am not a member of the council. My husband is the member." Baba drew himself up to appear very tall and said, "Swami gives you permission to ask your question." With this reassurance I proceeded to ask the question, at which he smiled sweetly and looking around at the gathering said approvingly, "That is a very good question, isn't it?"

He then answered it in such a clear and simple way that I have never forgotten his reply. He advised us to take one of his photographs and go alone to a quiet place, look at his likeness, and from our heart ask to be given an answer. He assured us that the answer would come within twenty minutes. However, we may not always be aware enough to receive it until later, or it may take longer to reach us, but it will always come. I have shared this advice with many people, and have used it myself on many occasions with success. So that is what I did to determine what should be done in this current situation, whether to attend the conference or go to Baba's birthday. All I wanted to know was where I would be the most useful.

The answer appeared to be definite that I should not attend the conference and should be at the ashram for the birthday. I must mention that it would never have occurred to me to decline to attend the conference had the organizer not asked me if I would like to do so. I also know that I really had no personal preference either way. I have never liked to be in large crowds. The festivals at the ashram, particularly Baba's birthday, always attract huge numbers of visitors, so I had been rather thankful that by arriving later, most of the crowds would have dispersed. Besides, I had already been at the ashram at a festival time twice that year, once for Chinese New Year and again for Guru Purnima.

I still worried that perhaps my mind was intruding in this decision, so I asked a couple of friends to erect a Maypole with me and ask to be guided to help decide between two courses of action. They each received the same answer, despite the fact that they both felt strongly that a promise should be kept once it has been made. With this decision I again spoke to the organizer to determine if he had any misgivings, or if he had changed his mind after asking me if I wished to withdraw. He was most gracious and even told me that if he were in my shoes he would cancel the conference and go to the birthday. Despite his reassurance I was still painfully aware that once again I would be in the unenviable position of causing the people who had expected to attend my lecture and workshop disappointment, possibly anger, and definitely surprise and criticism that I had broken my promise.

This time I had to come to a decision without the outside help I had been given on the two earlier occasions. Once again I was put through the turmoil of indecision, knowing what the effect would be if I withdrew. But again, l was forced to make it, despite what effect it would have.

When I asked within at the time of the second cancellation of the visit to Belgrade about the effect on the people who would be disappointed, the answer I was given was that if I made the right decision that was my sole responsibility; I must leave the people in Baba's care, for he knew why this had to happen. So the same must surely apply in this latest case. But for someone who has always had a horror of hurting or disappointing others, it was an extremely difficult decision to make and one over which I truly suffered until it was made. Only then could I relax and leave the result to Baba or the Hi C.

Hopefully, yet another patch has been emptied of its life and energy, and the karma worked out so that it will be easier to face other similar decisions when they arise in the future.

Most of us want to please others and have them like and admire us. But this can lead to the point where we allow them and their wishes to control us, in which case we cannot follow our own guidance from the Hi C, which may be contrary to their expectations. We are afraid that we will antagonize others and lose their friendship. But to be free, we have to cut the ties to the atmosphere that accumulated around the topic of pleasing our parents, or elders, or other authority figures, and thus not following the guidance of our own Hi C.

The above examples illustrate the need to say "No" when groups, rather than individuals, are involved. But we are confronted daily with innumerable situations where we are faced with the necessity to make a decision, often having very little time to make a correct one.

In order to avoid a hasty decision that is invariably based on old habit patterns, I have learned from such experiences to say that I would prefer not to give an immediate answer until I've had time to think or meditate on it. At first, other people will tend to balk at such a position, especially if they are intent on bending us to their will. But, if we can remain firm in our refusal to be pressured for an immediate answer, they will eventually become used to our new stance, and in some cases, will even gain more respect for us.

It is helpful to watch for those occasions when we are being asked to do something and feel obligated to come to a decision, but later regret it, and wish we had been given more time and less pressure to provide an answer. There are several ways we can avoid similar situations in the future. We can quickly reply that we need more time to consider the various implications and cannot be rushed into a decision. In time, people will hesitate to create such awkward situations when they see that we are taking more responsibility for our own actions and can no longer be coerced. Our reputation as a pushover will have changed.

However, we are often influenced by guilt, and we acquiesce rather than risk being left with an uncomfortable sense of guilt if we fail to go along with other people's demands. This guilt could have its origin in childhood, or have been brought over from a past life. Whatever the cause, it is a waste of time and energy, and needs to be released by means of the Wet Suit Exercise outlined at the end of this chapter. In addition, remember that we alone are responsible for our life and no one else has the right to decide for us. We will have to take the consequences for our decisions, for no one else will be willing or able to do so for us.

Another useful exercise is to cut the ties to a symbol for the attitude in the family around decision making, for we are all influenced by the atmosphere around many topics during our formative years, and we carry these habits with us into later life. More examples of family patterns are given in other chapters.

Before we can cut these ties, we should examine the patterns that each of our parents have copied or inherited from their parents. How did they handle decision making? Were we allowed and even encouraged to make our own decisions, or did our parents make them for us? Did your mother and father have different ways to make decisions, so that you received conflicting models? Were you ever allowed to say "No"? Did they change their stand on certain issues so you were never sure what they wanted from you? All these are habits that you may have adopted or rebelled against, and you need to clarify them so you can cut the ties to those that do not support you in your right to make up your own mind what you do or don't do.

You may be given a symbol for your particular pattern as soon as you start to question the models you were given as a child. If not, you can either draw a symbol, or make a model from clay, by concentrating your conscious mind on an absorbing activity and using your weaker hand to draw the symbol or make a model of it. After two weeks of practicing the Figure Eight (refer to the end of chapters on "Roles as Patches" and "The Family Atmosphere" for the Figure Eight Exercises), the symbol can be destroyed in whatever way is indicated by the Hi C. This simple exercise is most effective in helping to release from all unwanted patterns. Freedom to say "No" is the result.

EXERCISE 2
USING THE WET SUIT TO REMOVE GUILT

Guilt is a constricting emotion and can be likened to a black rubber wet suit that is worn by surfers.

Imagine you are wearing a tight black rubber wet suit that covers your entire body.

Ask the Hi C to indicate a specific guilt you are carrying from some negative action, thought, or feeling you expressed at some time in your life.

Ask how you can make amends for whatever you did, thought, or felt that caused you to feel guilty.

Remove the wet suit either all in one piece or in small strips or pieces, and make a pile of them.

Ask the Hi C how you should destroy the pile. It can be burned, dropped into acid, buried, or destroyed some other way. Make sure that every scrap has been destroyed.

Ask to be shown a body of water in which to take a cleansing bath, and scrub your entire body to free it from guilt.

Express your freedom from guilt in any way you please, as you expose your whole body to the air and sunlight.

Go to a favorite tree to find your new raiment and put it on.

Thank the Hi C for your newfound freedom from guilt.

Return to full consciousness of the here and now.

Chapter 13

Physical Problems and Illnesses as Patches

I HAVE ALWAYS BEEN interested to know the various causes of physical illnesses because I have had my share of difficulties in this area most of my life. Not that any of them were life-threatening, but nevertheless they have been most frustrating, to say the least. Many different allergic reactions have headed the list and forced me to be more than normally aware of the food I eat, the clothes I wear, the air I breathe, the water I drink, and a host of other factors.

I entered into the search in past lives for the possible causes at a time when such investigation was not a common one, and I, myself, did not believe in the theory of karma and reincarnation. I had read about Edgar Cayce's remarkable ability to diagnose illnesses while in a trance state, and was eager to see if I could follow his example, though preferably not while in trance, which I did not feel comfortable in experiencing myself.

Although I have since come to the belief that it is not necessary to delve into the past in this way, for me, it appears to have been an important step to teach me what I had refused to accept, that this life is not the only one we have lived, and that what we are experiencing now may not have been caused by our conduct in this life. That insight itself, was a great relief to me.

During various past life regressions, I uncovered a life as a Jew and some of my physical problems were brought into this life as patches related to the karma derived from that particular former life. In addition to allergies and migraine headaches, I have also suffered from sciatica and attendant back pains, which evidently were also caused in that life.

When I originally reviewed the Jewish life, I decided that the impressions I was receiving could not possibly be correct. The man with whom I was identifying had apparently spent his entire life indulging in "wine, women, and song," which did not seem to be likely for a Jew at the time, with their strict laws. I subsequently read of a period when some Jews were Hellenized and adopted many of the current Greek practices. This man had ended his life paralyzed, and was unable to walk or take care of himself. But because he had led such a self-indulgent and selfish life, no one came forward to look after him in his time of great need, so he died lonely and helpless.

The many allergies I have inherited have prevented me from indulging in many kinds of food, as well as wine and liquor. Because so many items were deleted from my diet, food has never been particularly attractive or important for me other than to provide me with the necessary energy to carry on my daily life and work. As for promiscuity, I was married to my late husband for fifty-two years before he died, which speaks for itself.

I can only hope that I will have balanced that profligate life by the time I have come to the end of this life, hopefully having learned the lesson I missed then, by curtailing and controlling my appetites and desires that so strongly controlled me in the past.

It is the subconscious part of the mind in which all the old memories, habits, and desires are stored, not only from this life but from all our former ones. These old "tapes" have to be uncovered and eventually discarded, so that new habits can be initiated. We must weed out old habits and let go of them by practicing the Figure Eight (page 92) and cutting the ties that attach them to us so we can reprogram the subconscious. In order to do so, we must give the subconscious the correct message to bring about the desired changes, in a similar way to instructing a servant on how to put our house in order and keep it organized. One time, while I was working on this theme, the word *factotum* came into my mind. When I looked up the meaning in the dictionary, I found that it was described as a jack-of-all-trades, a handyman, or one who is able to accomplish all types of tasks, which is a perfect description of the role of the subconscious. We need to give it clear, simple, and specific directions for it to bring about the required changes. That involves identifying the old negative tapes that are to be released and destroyed before the new and more positive ones can replace them.

The conscious mind, with its limited capacity, must be given its correct role of a householder, with the subconscious as a servant or factotum who keeps the house in order. Then the right relationship between the conscious mind, the subconscious, and the Hi C, or superconscious, will be established, with the Hi C as the resident of the body or house while it is available during this lifetime. The Hi C is also ready to move on to a new abode when the present one is no longer habitable or of use to It.

Having mentioned the subject of allergies, I would like to discuss an interesting treatment for this problem that has come to my attention. It is called N.A.E.T. and was compiled by an Indian woman doctor, Dr. Devi S. Nhambudripad, DC, LAC, RN, OMD, Ph.D., author of the book, *Say Goodbye to Illness.** She discovered a way to reprogram the subconscious to release allergic reactions. Her method is very simple and noninvasive, and does not involve any type of medication to achieve positive results in terminating the reaction to various substances that formally produced allergic symptoms. One of her theories is that an allergic reaction can result if something traumatic happens at the same time someone is in contact with a substance. Apparently many psychosomatic conditions may be caused in this way.

For instance, if, while a child is eating a certain food, something upsetting occurs, such as a family quarrel or harsh criticism from the parents, the message that is instantly received and imprinted on the subconscious is that eating that food is dangerous, as it is linked to an unpleasant happening.

Food is not the only thing that triggers allergic reactions. People, animals, certain types of clothes, and many, many other things can be the cause if connected in the subconscious to some kind of unpleasant or painful incident. The subconscious is not rational like the conscious mind, so everything that it registers remains intact unless and until it is uncovered and released.

---

*Published in 1993 (Buena Park, CA: Delta Publishing Co.). To contact them if you can't find the book in local bookstores, write 7282 Melrose St., Suite F, Buena Park, CA, 90621.

CHAPTER 14

BLOOD TYPES AS
PATCHES OR MAGNETS

ANOTHER INTEREST-
ing theory recently presented is *4 Blood Types: 4 Diets* by
Dr. Peter D'Adamo.* His father conducted research into the
possibility that each blood type requires certain specific
foods while others should be avoided for optimum health.
He suggests that according to our ancestral line at birth we
acquired a particular blood type, O, A, B, or AB. And that—
depending on our blood type—we need to eat foods that
are compatible with that type. The author lists each kind
of food and indicates which ones are acceptable, which are
neutral, and which should be avoided for each of the four
blood types.

I was most interested in his theory, particularly as the
foods he recommends for my blood type, as well as those
he listed as detrimental, were already known to me from
many years of experimenting with my diet requirements.
But perhaps the most interesting point was that those people with type O blood cannot thrive on a vegetarian diet.

*Peter D'Adamo, *4 Blood Types: 4 Diets* (New York: G.P. Putnam's Sons, 1996).

Many years ago, when my late husband and I were in an interview with Sai Baba, he deliberately turned his back on me to face my husband and told him he must make sure his wife eats fish and chicken. I was so startled by this that I blurted out, "But Baba." I got no further, for he wheeled around to face me and said with great severity, "You heard what Swami said." In a way I was not as surprised by what he actually said as by the fact that he should have said it, since he has always advocated that his devotees become strict vegetarians. However, in my case, I have tried to be a vegetarian several times in my life, but have always become very weak and lacking in energy and enthusiasm. The reason for this reaction is that I am allergic to most of the alternate sources of protein, such as dairy products, anything made from soybeans, most of the pulses like dhal, so I could not derive sufficient protein to remain healthy. In one way it was a relief to have Baba verify what I had suspected, that I should eat fish and chicken, which I have done since that interview.

Several years later, I had to have a blood test, and to my surprise, the doctor involved asked if I was a vegetarian. When I told him I ate fish and chicken, he said he was glad, for he suspected that my blood type was the one that could not do well without animal protein. When the test results came back, they verified his suspicion. A few years later, when having another blood test, again to my surprise the doctor asked the same question—was I a vegetarian? Baba was, as usual, right again.

Just before I read the book on blood types I was surprised to find a quote from Baba in a talk given by Jack Hislop, the president of the Sri Sathya Sai Organization in the U.S.A. at that time, when he was in Auckland, New Zealand, just before he died. He was asked about eating meat. Here is what he said. "Swami is an eminently reasonable person and is perfectly aware that sick people need strong vitamins like mutton and chicken. In fact, the metabolism of a number of people is such that if they do not have meat proteins they get terribly sick, waste away and die. They have to have meat protein to survive. If your doctor tells you, for example, that you need animal proteins, then follow your doctor's instructions. Dedicate it to Swami. Say, 'Swami, I am following my doctor's instruction, I dedicate the eating of this food to Thyself. Please, carry the burden, Swami, not me.' Put the burden on the Lord."

Dr. Adamo's book has explained the reason for these statements. Considering that it is a proven fact that a person with one type of blood cannot accept a transfusion of a different type, it is no wonder that each blood type thrives on different foods.

Here again, is another patch, for we have drawn to us the blood type we needed to inherit from the long line of ancestors in the family into which we were born. A certain type is peculiar to each of us; we do not all share the same one. We have to accept the indications that go along with our own blood type without being fanatical and insisting on a diet that is not harmonious for us, or that will not provide us with the energy we must have to learn from this life's experiences. When we lack energy it is extremely difficult to do whatever is necessary to face the various tests along the way. It takes great strength to avoid the temptation to run away from difficulties by turning to an addiction, such as alcohol or drugs, that we hope will provide relief, however temporary. Even sleep can be an escape from whatever we have attracted to us on our path. The same applies to television or any other pursuit that distracts us from facing one day at a time and asking the Hi C to help us deal with the various events we draw to us for our own progress.

I have often observed that those people who do not eat correctly often overeat in an attempt to adjust to their inadequate diet. This is particularly true of many vegetarians who ingest large amounts of sugar and carbohydrates to supply the energy they need, which they are not receiving if their diet is not in accord with their blood type.

PART III

ROLES AND KARMA

CHAPTER 15

ROLES AS PATCHES

HOW DO THE PATCHES we bring in with us affect the many varied roles we play? Sometimes, if a role in a past life was extremely strong, we are apt to continue to play it in the present life, whether it is appropriate or not. For instance, if we were extremely controlling at some time in the past, we may find it difficult to drop that role the next time around. We may try to continue to assume control in circumstances—and with people or situations—that prevent us from exerting the same kind of control this time as we were able to do previously. This will cause frustration until we realize that to continue this behavior brings only more problems instead of the apparent success we achieved in the past.

Gradually, as we continue to observe our attitude, we may learn that it is not conducive to our well-being to continue to try to dominate either situations or people. We will be forced to change as we meet with opposition. If the control in the past life was intense, it may take a long time and involve many hard knocks before we are able to let go of the old pattern and become more cooperative with others. Sometimes, when the old pattern is still strongly imprinted, it takes several lifetimes for intensely controlling people to release the old way of behaving. Some lives may have to be lived under the extreme control of someone else. We might be born to an extremely dominating parent to experience what it is like to be so helpless under his or her control. Or we may have a debilitating illness, or some physical condition, such as paralysis or something equally crippling, whereby we are controlled, not by a person but by the condition that leaves us helpless. In this way, we may find ourselves in situations similar to ones we may have inflicted on others in the past. Hopefully, we will begin to learn how very painful it is to be so dominated and decide never to repeat that old pattern again. In this way, slow steps are taken in the learning process if some kind of physical condition exerts the control. For instance, if we inflicted physical abuse on others in the past, we could well be the recipient of similar abuse now, to enable us to experience what we once did to others.

It is useless to blame other people, God, or fate for our present lives. We ourselves have caused our present condition, and we can remove it by reversing the old negative behavior and replacing it with a more positive attitude.

Each patch in this patchwork quilt of personality we bring with us represents an aspect that was not exhausted from one of our previous lives. It is brought over to form a small part of this present one. We can use this patch as an aid with which to learn something as yet not understood or accepted. As we painstakingly use up the energy remaining in the many various patches, the quilt will fall to pieces when the energy that kept it alive is no longer available. The quilt is like a map of the labyrinth through which we journey toward the light. We can eventually identify with the Hi C instead of with the body/mind/personality/ego which we mistakenly believe to be who we are. I repeat, it is not always necessary or even advisable to know all the details of the past lives from which the patches originated, for that knowledge could lead to the past experience being etched anew.

We only need to use each patch to free us from the old karma attached to it by learning whatever it was that we failed to learn before. Of course, many of us are completely unaware of the fact that we have such a quilt, in which case it will be gradually de-energized on an unconscious level and in certain cases not at all. When that is the case, we will be forced to re-enter Earth life and be given another opportunity to reduce the number of patches we carry with us. It is obvious that this is a slow and laborious process!

If we consciously choose to ascertain the meaning of the patches, and are willing to work on them instead of wasting time and energy in lamenting our harsh fate, painful situation, or difficult relationships, we can hasten the whole process and be free from the results of our past actions. In order to start such a process, we begin by making a conscious effort to remove the patches. Our entire life is like a mirror in which is reflected all those parts that still carry energy or life force, and the various roles we assume now can show us how we may have behaved in the past.

The personality is composed of the many different roles we have assumed, each one representing a patch that indicates the various aspects on which to work. Some of these aspects of personality are good and we leave them alone. Some of these aspects (or patches) make us feel uncomfortable with ourselves. They may be the patches to concentrate on when beginning to remove the karmic ones.

A considerable number of people fall into one of two categories; those who habitually dominate others, and those who have come under their control. This type of relationship can be compared to a master and slave, or a rug and the one who walks on the rug. These two roles lock the two participants involved into a tight codependent relationship from which it is difficult to break free. This is one patch to consider. Does it belong in your quilt?

All roles obviously do not apply to everyone. We all play many roles, so we have to detect the ones that control us. It is difficult, and in some cases impossible, to extricate ourselves from our various role playing. If it brings pain, it might be a patch.

Most of the roles we play are described in greater detail in my book *Cutting More Ties That Bind*. The two common ones that follow will supply examples to show how to recognize them. Once a patch has been recognized, we can learn how to free ourselves from it by using the Figure Eight.

EXERCISE 3
FIGURE EIGHT: CUTTING TIES FROM PEOPLE

The Figure Eight is a symbol that enables people to protect their own territory or space and at the same time, avoid invading anyone else's space. It is advisable to have only one person or other controlling factor at a time in the circle opposite your own when practicing the Figure Eight Exercise, to avoid confusing your separate reactions to different people or other controlling factors. An exception to this rule is when you wish to cut the ties to a group, such as a work force you are leaving, or a religious, political, or other organization that has exerted control over you and so prevents you from being able to follow the guidance of the Hi C.

Two weeks is the minimum time for practicing the Figure Eight prior to a cutting of the ties. This provides the time necessary to allow the projections or influence of one person or object over the other to be withdrawn. In some cases you may find that even more time is needed before you feel you are ready to proceed with a cutting of the ties.

To practice the Figure Eight, imagine you are sitting or standing in a circle of golden light on the ground around your feet. The radius of this circle is the length of your arms with the fingers extended.

Visualize another circle of golden light directly in front of you. It is about the same size as yours and just touching, but it doesn't overlap your circle.

Starting at the point where the two circles touch, visualize a neon blue light flowing in a clockwise direction around the opposite circle to a point where they meet.

Continue to let it flow around the left side of your circle, around your back, around your right side and back to where the two circles touch, to form a Figure Eight.

Continue to visualize the Figure Eight of neon blue light for two minutes at a time, as you awaken in the morning, again as you are about to go to sleep at night, and whenever you have time during the day.

This symbol, and others, are clearly explained and illustrated in the *Cutting the Ties That Bind Workbook*, for those who would like to be more involved in the work.

CHAPTER 16

THE DOORMAT ROLE

A VERY COMMON ROLE that is extremely hampering is the role of the doormat. It is not only a serious problem for those who have, for some reason, assumed it, but it is equally detrimental to the people who tie into it by walking all over the "doormat." Each participant enables the other to continue being controlled by a role, in this case, either a doormat or the one who treats all those who allow it, as doormats.

There are many different reasons for this role. One is karmic, for it is probable that at some previous time the people who are now acting as doormats previously walked roughshod over others, with no consideration for other people's welfare or wishes. What better way to learn the lesson involved here than by having to experience the very same treatment that was meted out in the past to others? Only by suffering in the present whatever we were guilty of doing to others in the past, can we realize how painful it was for those we treated in such an unkind and thoughtless way.

We do not necessarily need to become acquainted with all of the precise details of the past life. Merely recognizing the probable reason for our present role is usually a sufficient incentive to be willing to correct it. We cannot change the past as it is gone, but we can certainly try to learn from it in the present, as that is the only option we have available that can thus influence the future.

As soon as we accept the responsibility for the past errors of our ways, we are in a position to stop perpetuating either of the roles and this, in turn, will help everyone who has taken advantage of us by treating us like doormats.

In line with the concept of karma, we are born into a family that makes it possible for us to play this role, even if it appears to have been thrust upon us. But whatever the many roles we have played and whatever the reason, our only recourse is to extract the lesson embedded in each role, accept it, learn what we can, and then discard it.

Another cause for assuming the doormat role is an overwhelming need to be liked, loved, or approved, and accepted by others. Actually, the opposite is often the result, for those who walk all over others are more likely to despise their victims as weak and therefore beneath their approval, let alone their love. They continue their arrogant attitude purely for their own convenience, with no consideration for the person they so abuse.

Interestingly enough, as soon as the doormats assert themselves, their partners in this role playing will invariably react very strongly at the onset of a change and will try every means in their power to prevent any alteration in the behavior patterns and try to bring the relationship back to its original state. This is a critical time for the recovering doormat, when a great deal of courage and fortitude is called for, to avoid reverting back to the original role.

As with all such changes, if we can stay firm but calm, and clearly—with a minimum of emotion—state our own right to become free from roles that are restricting our freedom to express our own nature, the opposer will invariably listen, due to surprise or even shock at the change in our reaction. The result, however, may well be the loss of the relationship, which is actually no real loss compared to the lack of freedom imposed by the role.

Another benefit to releasing the role is that as soon as it is no longer acting as a magnet to draw to us those people who will enable us to continue to play it, we will begin to discover our own strength. This strength can be developed by allowing the Hi C to use us as Its instruments, employing any role that is appropriate and timely.

As with all other attachments, a symbol for this role must be found and then visualized in the opposite circle of the Figure Eight (page 92) for at least two weeks, often longer. At the end of that time, the circles are to be separated and the symbol for the role destroyed. The circle that contained the symbol is erased. To finish the process, if a picture or a clay model of the role was made, it also has to be destroyed, to give the subconscious a strong message that the role will no longer be assumed.

CHAPTER 17

THE CONTROLLER ROLE

MOST OF US HAVE A
horror of insecurity, especially of not being in control of
our lives, and we will go to great lengths to hold on to it.
Sai Baba has a saying that he often repeats in an attempt to
have this message register. It is, "Love my uncertainty,"
which is quite frightening for many people to accept, let
alone to live accordingly. He also gives another directive
that is equally unnerving to many people: "Abandon your
plans, even the best ones."

But if we truly comprehend that we are not the body or
the will, ego, or personality, then both of these sayings make
excellent sense.

When we earnestly set out to be an instrument of the
Hi C, one of the chief requisites is to be willing to relinquish
our own idea of how we can be used and allow the Hi C to
guide us to be at the right place at the correct time, with
whoever is present, so that It can use us in whatever way is
the most helpful, not just for us, but for everyone concerned. To repeat, Surrender, Trust, and Accept is a much

needed daily exercise to help us give up our attempted control by the ego so we can accept the guidance of the Hi C. At first, this new approach can, for many of us, be extremely frightening and can cause an intense feeling of insecurity. But, as we become accustomed to it we will find that its effect is very freeing, and we will automatically stop worrying about the future and be ready to live fully in the present, one minute at a time, by asking the Hi C to supply us with sufficiently clear signs to indicate the steps we should take.

Whether we accept either the role of master or slave, in each one we are actually being controlled by someone or something other than the Hi C. The person who plays the master is controlled by his or her ego/will and the slave by someone else's ego/will.

In this work, we have been taught that no one has the right to exert control over anyone else, for the simple reason that we are responsible only for our own growth and learning. We cannot learn for another person, even our own children; neither can we grow for them. We may like to believe that we know what is best for ourselves, but that is not always the case, as many of us find out the hard way and to our surprise and pain, when things do not turn out the way we expected. So, since we cannot always know what we ourselves need, how can we possibly know what is right for someone else? Therefore, to try to control someone else is a veritable ego trip, for to do so implies that we know what is best for that person. However, most of the time we are more concerned with what will meet our own needs and arrogantly demand that those people we have reduced to being our "slaves" supply these needs.

Most instances of control are obvious, but there are also more subtle types of control. For instance, some people use illness or a disability to keep other family members in the role of slaves who are expected to care for them.

Others will try to control another person by withholding love if that person is not willing to comply with some demand. Some people have a habit of making another feel guilty if he or she is not willing to go along with demands made or by accusing another of neglect or a lack of love. Others assume a sweet attitude to cover up the control they wish to exert and appear hurt when they are confronted with it. Many people use money to gain control over others, especially family members or those who are in a position of dependence. There are countless ways by which people attempt to exert control, so we all must investigate the often subtle ways we behave with other people to gain what we believe we want another to provide for our benefit.

PART IV
FAMILY KARMA

CHAPTER 18

THE FAMILY ATMOSPHERE

In the first book, *Cutting the Ties That Bind,* I suggested that we make two lists: one for the father and one for the mother. Each list is divided into two columns, one to include all the positive traits of each parent and in the other all the negative ones. The original reason for these lists of parental attributes was to determine whether we had either copied one or the other, or rebelled and acted in as opposite a way as possible. The young of all species learn by mimicking their parents' behavior. However, human children are able either to copy or rebel according to how they react to each parent.

Each one of us comes into this present life wearing our invisible patchwork quilt, composed of all the traits that block us from knowing who we are. This prevents us from allowing the Real Self to use our personality with its traits, attributes, and all the other parts of our human self as Its instrument.

Since we have been shown that each patch still retains our energy from past actions, we are born into an environment that will allow us the opportunity to unravel the various patches so they no longer contain our energy and cease to control us and attach us to the physical sheath instead of the Hi C.

So we need to enter the world again as a baby, either male or female, and into a family with all the combined heritage of the two parents, together with the personalities of all the family members, for our learning. All these individuals are our potential teachers, but only if we can accept them as such, instead of rejecting them—and with them, all they can teach us.

In addition to the relatives and close associates, we are introduced into a family situation containing many different types of atmosphere around innumerable subjects that we ingest just as we breathe in air. All of these act as barriers to our contact with the Hi C and our acceptance of It as our guide. As we remove these blocks we begin to reveal the light within, so that It can shine forth and add Its luster to help illuminate the world and bring back the lost heart that has been missing for centuries. In this way, as we achieve our own personal release, we also contribute to the emergence of the world from the present darkness into light, from hatred and warfare to love and compassion. It is therefore a privilege—as well as a necessity—to be involved in working on our personal release, and at the same time helping to bring balance into the world.

In addition to the release from authority and security figures, the many varied atmospheres around innumerable subjects that prevailed in the home in which we were raised and permeated our life, needs to be uncovered and released. We were literally immersed in this complex culture very much like fish in the water that surrounds them. We must clearly see our reactions to all of them so we can be in a

position to determine whether we are free to express ourselves now in the way we would choose were we able to do
so.

Reactions do not necessarily denote true beliefs, and are
often outdated or inappropriate in our present life, even
though they may have been relevant during childhood. A
major part of becoming mature involves determining how
we were programmed around various subjects. Then we can
consider whether or not the concepts we adopted truly represent the attitude we want to express now that we have at-
tained adulthood. How do they fit in with the beliefs to
which we wish to adhere and practice, or are they in conflict
with our beliefs?

As soon as we have uncovered the main subjects that triggered a strong reaction in us, we can release their hold over
us. The more strongly our parents held on to old beliefs, the
more they would try to force us to accept them, and the
more force they would use, the more we would rebel. But
it's no longer necessary to continue to have these reactions.
It's far preferable to cut the ties to old patterns that are no
longer useful so we are free to decide how we really want to
live.

The original lists of the parents' attributes prove to be
even more helpful in indicating the patterns from which we
need to be detached. When we are free from their control,
we can begin to express whatever is valid and useful for us
as individuals, instead of following unconsciously in the
footsteps of parents who have a different karmic heritage.

Each of us came into this life with specific patches, but
no two people have identical ones, any more than they have
identical fingerprints. Since each patch still retains our energy from past actions, we choose to be born into an environment that will allow us the opportunity to unravel the

various patches so they no longer contain our energy and cease to control us.

The patches therefore draw us to a family appropriate for our learning, one that contains within it the very challenges we must face and overcome in order to develop into suitable instruments for the Hi C to use.

We want to examine the influence of early programming around a wide variety of subjects. As children, in most cases, we accepted the concepts expressed by parents and relatives as true and meaningful. Some undoubtedly were, while others were, perhaps, useful at the time when we were children, but are inappropriate for the present situation. Many beliefs and practices are handed down from one generation to the next. Some stem from the cultural background of the family, or the customs of the country or national group into which we were born. We have imbibed them along with our mother's milk mostly on an unconscious level, without any conscious consideration of whether they were valid or even useful. They cover almost every possible topic and are woven into the developing personality that covers our true identity.

Since they were passed on to us by parents and other family or group members, and did not originate from within, we now want to ascertain whether they are true or useful for us at the present time in our lives. If not, we must cut the ties that attach them to us and let go of them. When they are still a part of our personality, even though we may still be unconscious of their existence, they will continue to influence everything we do. They constitute a belief system, or set of precepts, by which we have lived by automatically following them. Each one is a thought form that has grown into a habit that controls our behavior.

These family habits are frequently the cause of other people's attitude toward us. Because we are invariably unconscious of our habits and behavior, we are often bewildered when we evoke reactions in others that we do not feel we deserve.

We all grow up in a distinctive atmosphere, or family climate, that we bring with us into our adult life. Now that this concept has been brought to our attention, it is also obvious that we are actually reacting to the "climate" around many different subjects, just as the parents reflect the atmosphere in which they were raised. Again, we see a chain reaction from one generation to the next. This is actually our "inheritance" from our family.

Since the family climate or atmosphere is a thought form, it has been supplied with energy by members of the family, sometimes over a long period of time, so it has become very strong. In fact, it can be so powerful that children raised in it are usually overwhelmed, and find it impossible to break free from its control.

In order to uncover some of these early "climates," we must engage in a veritable search similar to a treasure hunt to find the clues that are buried in the past. The most obvious reason for this laborious undertaking is that until its influence on our life has been brought to our attention, we remain unaware of its existence.

This search requires that we be willing to take a journey of discovery back in memory. We must ask the Hi C to show us the many and varied belief systems formed by the psychological atmosphere into which we were born, and continued during our years with our family, because it still exerts an influence over us to the present day.

One useful way to discover acquired family attitudes is with the help of self-inquiry. To what subjects do I react very strongly? Do I have rigid ideas concerning politics, and become very forceful in expressing my views and preferences, and am I intolerant of other peoples' point of view? What is my approach to religion? Do I allow those who espouse a different affiliation to express their beliefs without becoming irate or critical, or without trying to persuade them to accept my different point of view, which I, of course, consider to be superior to theirs? Another subject that is fraught with strong reactions involves raising children and education in general. Where did I acquire my opinions and are they valid or even relevant?

There is also another possibility. Do I become overly upset, feel insecure, or defensive when I am in the company of someone who is expressing very strong views on a particular subject? If so, what happened during my childhood to cause me to react in that way now? Did my father or mother, or other close relatives, project onto me very strong views with which I was forced to agree despite my own personal conviction that they were not correct? In addition, was I punished whenever I disagreed with whatever they were propounding? Or, was I made the butt of their ridicule or hostility for my contrary stance? All of these old conditions are thought forms that strongly influence us and must be removed if we are to be free to go within to determine what our own authority, the Hi C, will teach us is appropriate action.

However, inherited attitudes to innumerable subjects are not necessarily negative as such. It is only when they have become too controlling that they should be released so we can be free to make direct contact with the source within. Then, with the Hi C's help, we will discover the correct attitude toward each of the many things that affect our lives and require us to make decisions on how best to deal with them. If we allow old patterns, either inherited or learned from parents, other relatives, or peers to control us, we will never be free to express what is correct for us as individuals.

This individuation process will eventually free us, and we will realize that by releasing or detaching from all the exterior factors, we will be left with the kernel of our being—the Real Self—at which level we will be one with all other Selves. (See Exercise 4.) Thus, we move away from control by other people's egos in order to arrive at the point where we know, without a doubt, that as we are God at the core of our being, so is everyone else. We are indeed all one. So we have to move away from family or tribal beliefs and practices to allow the Hi C to manifest through each of us. This will eventually lead to the Golden Age.

EXERCISE 4
FIGURE EIGHT: CUTTING TIES TO OBJECTS AND INTANGIBLES

The method for cutting the ties to a controlling factor other than a human being is different from the original cutting the ties ritual to a person. Sometimes it is difficult to find a symbol to represent something as intangible as an atmosphere or climate, so two possible methods can be used. For either one, an activity that completely engages your conscious mind is essential, such as watching television, reading an engrossing book, or listening to favorite music.

The first method involves the use of a sheet of paper and a pen, pencil, or crayons. If you are right-handed, use your left hand and vice versa. Ask the Hi C to guide your hand to make a drawing that will represent the climate or atmosphere from which you wish to be free, but bear in mind that you don't need to be an artist to produce a work of art or even a recognizable image. Your subconscious will understand the message and act accordingly.

Practice the Figure Eight for two weeks, or longer if necessary. Place your drawing in the circle opposite your own. At the end of this practice, ask the Hi C how to separate the two circles and how to destroy the symbol representing the family atmosphere. Then actually destroy the picture you have drawn to further impress the subconscious that you do not want to be controlled by it any longer.

The other method involves the use of modeling clay. The conscious mind again has to be distracted in some way by engaging in your chosen engrossing activity. Ask the Hi C to help you to make a model from a piece of clay to represent the atmosphere or climate from which you wish to free yourself. You can use both hands for the modeling, but as with the drawing, you don't have to create a masterpiece. Ask the Hi C how to destroy it and proceed to follow the instructions It gives. There are many ways to destroy the symbol. It can be given to an authority figure, such as your chosen personification of the Hi C, or some other personal choice. It can be burned, thrown into a volcano, buried, tossed into the ocean, or one of many other possibilities to impress your subconscious that you do not wish to be under its control any longer.

CHAPTER 19

ABOUT MONEY

W<small>E ALL HAVE OUR IN-</small>dividual approaches to money, depending upon the way our parents and other family members viewed that commodity. In some families, money becomes a security symbol. The children grow up feeling secure only if they think they have enough money, and lose their sense of security if at any time in their lives they are without it. It is a well-known fact that a collapse in the stock market is often accompanied by an increase in suicides. The same thing can be observed when gamblers lose money at the roulette wheel or crap table. Sometimes this attachment to money can lead to a kind of worship, akin to that directed to a deity.

This occurs when people endow money with the supernatural power to bring its owners happiness, security, acceptance, love, or any other boon they crave. They use money to bargain for whatever they desire. All efforts are directed toward acquiring as much money as possible, and they dread the very thought of losing it, so they strive to hold on to it and focus attention on adding more and more, never satisfied that there is enough. Since making as much money as possible is the goal, everything they do is designed to further this aim, however unrealistic it may be. In this case, the motive for work is not primarily to give service, but to add to the hoard. Such people also evaluate other people according to how wealthy they happen to be and feel vastly superior to those who are less affluent than themselves.

Then there are those who have been reared in a family where the parents were afraid to spend money, preferring to save it for a rainy day or, like misers, hoard it. Meanwhile, they penalize themselves and their children by skimping on food, clothes, shelter, and all the other basic necessities that money can buy.

There are many other different attitudes toward money. Each one of us needs to look back to when we were children and try to recall how money was presented to us by our parents. We might discover that there were conflicting ideas about money. Such a situation can occur when parents came from dissimilar backgrounds. In that case, they would each bring to the marriage whatever attitude toward money their parents held. Their children would inherit conflicting ideas, which could lead to difficulty in making correct decisions about money.

Suppose you were born into a family in which the mother brought to the partnership a tendency to be a spendthrift. On the other hand, the father had been raised to be very frugal. These two very different approaches would most certainly cause a great deal of friction between the parents. In turn, the conflict would rebound onto the children who would be torn between two opposing ways of handling money. Some of the children might follow the mother's example; while others would follow the father's, and some could be so confused by this contradiction that they would not be able to make a decision, and would tend to be alternately either too frugal or too extravagant.

Another destructive use of money which is extremely hard on the children, occurs when money is used as a threat or a bribe, and in this way is given too much power to control others. The children either resent being the recipient of the threats or bribes, or accept this behavior and act in a similar fashion, thus repeating the mistakes of the parents with their own children.

One young man with whom I was working was born to parents whose attitude toward money was very different. His father also had parents whose ideas were opposite from one another. The effect on the father was that sometimes he could be too generous and would spend too much for the wrong reasons. At other times he would be penurious to the point of being stingy. His children were never sure which action their father would take, so they grew up with mixed messages. The young man with whom I was working reacted in a similar way to his father by alternating between being a spendthrift and a miser.

The mother had been reared in a family where there was rarely enough money to supply their needs, so she brought to the marriage a fear of being penniless. One of the siblings followed her example, and tended to hoard money for a rainy day, while another one took the path of being extravagant.

As I was working only with the young man, I concentrated on helping him observe his erratic behavior. When he saw that the cause lay with the atmosphere in which he was raised, he was able to let go of his conflicting reactions and decide for himself what his approach should be, according to the particular circumstances facing him.

After he had practiced the Figure Eight for the required two-week period, using a symbol to represent his behavior pattern connected to money, he cut the ties that attached him to it. In his case, the result was immediate. He had suffered so much from the results of his erratic decisions regarding money that he was overjoyed to be given a method to help him to remove its effect. He also realized that he would, from now on, cease handing on to his children a similar pattern. In this way, he was able to cut the chain reaction brought down in his family and break free from its control over his use of money.

Another example involves a woman whose father was extremely controlling over every aspect of life. This attitude often stems from a feeling of insecurity, which was certainly true for this man. He had grown up with absolutely no security at all. He had been orphaned as a baby and sent to four different foster homes. When he became an adult, he developed an intense drive to control everyone and everything possible, in a desperate effort to counteract his early insecurity.

He judged people by how successful they were in terms of how much money they made, and criticized his wife and children continuously, calling them failures if they did not live up to his expectations. When I asked this woman for information about her mother, whom she rarely mentioned, she explained that the father was so controlling and had such a terrible temper that the mother was forced to follow the father's lead and was so brow-beaten that she died at an early age from sheer exhaustion and depression.

The daughter, who had been told constantly that she was acceptable only if she earned a large salary, entered the business world, hoping to gain her father's approval by being financially successful. However, she was not temperamentally suited to the life it involved, and was obliged to resign, which only added to her sense of failure. When she began to understand the reason for her dilemma, she cut the ties to her father's controlling pattern and was able to undergo training in a field more suited to her nature, and became successful in her own right. She is able to guide her children in a much more humane way than was her own experience.

Then there are those who were raised in a family where money was scorned as being beneath their notice. This group includes so-called spiritual people who maintain that it is not spiritual to possess a lot of money, and who therefore feel sullied whenever they are obliged to deal with it. However, they are often quite content to live off the money or "filthy lucre," as they refer to it, that their parents or others have earned. They apparently consider it their right to be supplied and have others support them, so that they are free from what they consider to be the soiling influence of money, and therefore a deterrent on the spiritual path if they themselves have any dealings with it. But, money is neutral, neither good nor bad of itself. It can have a negative or positive effect according to the motives of whoever is using it.

In some cases, instead of repeating a family pattern if it is too rigid, or makes you feel uncomfortable, you might act in an opposite way from other members of your family. Children born into a wealthy family often become rebellious and scoff at the way their parents revere money. Others, who have been brought up in a home where money was a scarcity will frequently try to make up for the early lack by striving to make as much money as possible in a compulsive effort to avoid repeating the family pattern of poverty and its effect on them. All of these patterns and many, many more are like a trap or prison that keeps each person chained to a particular limiting belief.

We all need to do our homework to discover for ourselves the climate or belief system around money in our family that has determined, to a large extent, our own attitude toward it, whether conscious or unconscious. We can then reprogram the subconscious, heal old traumas, and release the physical, mental, and emotional effects they have continued to exert on us.

In the past there have been many methods to help to reprogram the subconscious. The Coué method was one of the first, originated by Dr. Emile Coué. It was composed of affirmations that had to be repeated many times a day. One example was, "I am getting better and better every day in every way." However, it was found that after using it for a while, in some cases the reverse effect often occurred. My own observation has been that until we actually cut the ties to some of the old patterns, we cannot introduce new and more positive ones.

CHAPTER 20

ABOUT FOOD
AND DRINK

SINCE FOOD IS ONE OF
the main necessities to preserve life, many different myths
and beliefs have developed around it. Here again, children
absorb, on an unconscious level, the parents' attitude
toward food. If it is given too much importance in the family, the children will also attach undue importance to it.

As food supplies a feeling of comfort and satisfaction, it
is often used in times of stress, in an attempt to assuage fear,
anxiety, depression, or rejection. Such a habit can be so automatic that the person becomes addicted to food and relies
on it to supply whatever comfort or support is needed or
appears to be lacking. But neither food nor any other material substance can supply anything other than temporary relief. When its immediate affect fades, the same situation still
exists and must, at some point, be faced and resolved. So
this escape pattern that is often adopted in childhood in the
family must be released if the person has fallen under its
influence and has allowed it to limit the freedom to resolve
problems.

Another family habit connected to food occurs when food is used by parents as a bribe or a threat. In such cases, either the child is cautioned that if he or she does what the parent wishes, food will be given as a reward. Or, in reverse, if he or she disobeys the parent, certain favorite food items will be withheld.

This pattern often extends into other areas of life. For instance, some people feel the need to reward themselves with food for hard work or some accomplishment, especially if they were rewarded with food as children whenever they were successful. In this way, incorrect and actually harmful eating habits are established that can cause many different kinds of problems in adulthood, including bulimia and anorexia.

We therefore need to ascertain what specific pattern was connected to food, and find a symbol to represent it, since habits are intangible. It can then be visualized in the Figure Eight for at least two weeks before cutting the two circles apart and destroying the symbol. This sets us free from a childhood pattern that has continued to control our eating habits.

Another aspect of food is tied to the actual atmosphere around the table while eating. In many families, mealtime is seen as an opportunity to discuss problems and indulge in criticism. This custom links the very act of eating with unpleasant experiences, and causes tension connected with food and eating.

One family that comes to mind used mealtimes as an opportunity to have each member review the day's activities so that all their faults could be aired and discussed. This routine caused great tension in each of the members, and resulted in food and eating being equated with anxiety. Each of the siblings suffered from intestinal and stomach ailments until one or two of them cut the ties to old reactions and shared the possibility of release with the others.

In my own case, I was forced to finish every scrap of food on my plate before I was allowed to get up from the table. This practice was always accompanied by my being reminded of the starving Armenians. I did not have the slightest idea who they were, but they became my enemies because they were used to make me eat more than I could manage to ingest. It was not until I cut the ties to this early programming that mealtimes ceased to cause me tension.

To sum up, if food is too important to parents, it is frequently also very important to the children. If it is used as a bribe or reward, it will be used later in life as a reward for something, or as a comfort. If it is linked to love and approval, the children will turn to it whenever they feel unloved, criticized, or insecure. Binges and other eating disorders often have their origin in such family patterns.

CHAPTER 21

TIME AND PUNCTUALITY

I HAD NEVER BEFORE considered the fact that everyone in the world has exactly the same amount of time at their disposal until Sai Baba mentioned it to me in an interview. Yes, when we stop to think about it, we all have just 24 hours each day for our use. However, the way we decide to use our time depends, to a large extent, on the family attitude toward time, together with our own reactions to that early conditioning.

As with all other learning processes, we either copy or rebel against our parents' management of time. In addition to this early environment and its affect, some people seem to bring with them at birth their own habits, while others appear to have inherited family traits. In the latter case, there may be one family member who has a very different attitude toward time from the others in the same family. For instance, in a family where all the members are punctual, there may be one who, from early childhood, appears to be oblivious of time and is always late. Or, the reverse may be the case: one member is always punctual, while the rest of the family are invariably tardy. These two possibilities are not as common as those where the early conditioning determined which way the various members will react.

In a family where the father is a stickler for having everyone be punctual, some of the children might follow his example and always be on time. But if he happens to be too rigid or dictatorial, some of the more independent siblings will rebel against his strict control and deliberately flout his authority by always making sure they are late and thus keep him waiting. Neither of these reactions represents a correct approach, so it is helpful to cut the ties to whichever habit was adopted, to free ourselves from its control. Then the real solution, which is to be aware of inner timing, can be initiated.

Sai Baba made a point of this inner timing one time when my husband and I were sitting in his house in Whitefield awaiting his entrance. As he passed by where I was sitting, he quickly turned back toward me and pointed to the watch I was wearing, which has no numbers on the dial. He looked very pleased and said, "Very happy. Very happy. Inner time, not outer time." By referring to inner time I gathered that we should turn within to enable the Hi C to lead us to be at the right place at the right time.

I recall a song from the show, *My Fair Lady*, in which the father of the bride, who was afraid he would be late for the ceremony, ends the song with, "Get me to the church on time." I use this little jingle when I am caught in traffic and am not sure I will arrive at an appointment on time. But instead of church, I substitute the place where I am going. I am often surprised at how well it works, if only because it relaxes me.

When we consciously turn within and ask the Hi C to guide us in every aspect of our lives, everything begins to fall into place. We find that we are at the right place at the right time without the tension so often produced when we strain to bring about the same result with our own will.

One thing that really impressed me one day while in a reverie was the realization that when we are late for an appointment we are actually stealing from the person who is thus kept waiting, whether it is a friend, a business associate, or another professional contact. Whoever it may be, the person could be using the time being wasted while waiting for our arrival in a more productive way. So we are stealing that opportunity. Of course, there are occasions where we have no control over our arrival time. We may be trapped in traffic, or a bus, train, or plane could be late, in which case, we too, are being deprived of the chance to use the time in a more practical way. But such situations are not typical, and are also beyond our control, in which case we are not to blame for being late. It is the everyday need for punctuality that has to be addressed. Since our habits stem most often from early conditioning, we must find a suitable symbol to place in the other circle of the Figure Eight in preparation to detaching from this habit that has been controlling us.

Tardiness is only one aspect of time management. There are also those people who are driven to always be early. They allow twice as much time to arrive for an appointment and then have to cool their heels when the person they have arranged to meet has not arrived, is not yet available, or may even be late.

Either of these two extremes prevents a natural flow or rhythm, and causes frustration in those who are kept waiting, as well as those who arrive too early, or in both parties.

Some people try to cheat time by attempting to accomplish far too many tasks in too short a period of available time. This habit causes them to be repeatedly late, which, in turn makes them feel rushed and never able to relax. They report that if they can accomplish everything in as short a period as possible they can "beat the clock." Many car accidents and speeding tickets result from this tendency. We cannot compete with and beat time. We can try to flow with it and make a habit of asking the Hi C to help us to be at the right place at the right time and be able to accomplish only what It knows is necessary in any time period.

The more extreme reactions to time are triggered by parents in children when the parents are too rigid and controlling. When children grow up in a relaxed atmosphere, and are taught by the example of their parents, they invariably develop a comfortable attitude toward time—not too lax, but not too rigid either.

Chapter 22

Work Atmosphere

The work ethic has been rapidly changing throughout the world during recent years. Service to the community as the motive for work is fast disappearing. An attitude of "everyone for himself" is replacing it to a large extent in many work areas. What will benefit me? How much can I earn doing as little work as possible? These seem to be the usual responses to the question of choosing a career. Many people, especially young adults, seem to be of the opinion that the world owes them a living, so they do not need to take responsibility for themselves.

Complaints about the quality of work and the attitude of workers are more frequently heard. This mistaken work ethic is apparent in most countries, but particularly in the United States. The fact that many people from other countries tend to copy everything American, whether it is admirable or not, is spreading this problem. In addition, the peer pressure among young people is such that those who do not adhere to the current standards of the majority are ostracized, which few young people can tolerate.

This approach to work has, as the underlying cause, the thought form built up and sustained by greed. Greed rears its ugly head in all areas of activity, whether purely personal, or in the many public areas, such as commerce, politics, medicine, religion, education, communication and the media, the arts, food and supplements, fashion, and many others. It is like a virus that has infected people all over the world. Children growing up in this atmosphere catch the virus at a very early age when they observe their parents' behavior, for offspring of any species copy whatever role model they see.

Greed causes energy blocks. There is a natural rhythm to all systems which, if broken, results in a block to the natural flow of energy. This, in turn, creates stagnation. Greed causes certain people to acquire more than they need of any given thing and to continue to hold on to it and refuse to let go. Such attachment creates many different negative conditions whether of a physical, mental, or emotional nature.

Greed in the workplace has reached epidemic proportions and is the direct cause of limitless suffering. Those workers who are more aggressive and selfish push those who are less selfish out of their way so they can get ahead. This, in turn, frustrates those who are trying to live according to a more unselfish model, so they often wonder if their chosen lifestyle is worth the effort they expend on giving service as their chief intent, when it apparently earns little in return. From the outer view, it appears that the selfish and aggressive people are successful, and the more dedicated ones are the losers. This state of affairs is prevalent everywhere, but unless it changes, the escalating greed will lead to a collapse of the system that now supports our way of life.

What can we as individuals do to help? We can scrutinize our own attitude to determine how we acquired it and where it originated. What was the family attitude toward work? Were we encouraged to give our best effort to serving in whatever capacity our occupation warranted? Was work introduced as a necessary evil? Was either of our parents a workaholic? Did either consider work to be beneath them? Did either of our parents' work take them away from home so that we felt work was an enemy, preventing us from having attention and love? There are many different patterns that we have all absorbed on the subconscious level that affect our approach to work as adults. As soon as we have identified the particular message we received as children, we can find a symbol to express its hold on us and practice the Figure Eight (page 92) with it for the required two weeks. After this exercise, the circle containing the symbol can be cut away and the symbol destroyed. When we have freed ourselves from this overlay from childhood, we can determine the correct attitude we should adopt now.

CHAPTER 23

HEALTH AND SICKNESS

MANY PEOPLE HAVE absorbed various concepts around health and sickness on an unconscious level. These often originate in superstitions handed down from ancestral beliefs and old wives' tales that are no longer valid. These can exert a strong influence on family members by locking them into constricting patterns that cause fear if family members fail to act according to these constraints, which were even used as threats on occasion.

I recall one case in which a woman had been constantly warned during childhood that if she disobeyed her mother, it would cause the latter to have a heart attack or a stroke. Since there was obviously no way to prove or disprove such an assertion, she continued to register fear lest she be the cause of her mother's death whenever she found herself disagreeing with her mother. Consequently, she was obliged to obey her every wish. Such complete control had a stultifying effect on the child's future development and prevented her from being free to express any part of herself. This condition continued on into adulthood and paralyzed her to such an extent that she was fearful of going against anyone else's wishes, and always suppressed her own inclinations.

When she understood how she had been programmed in this way, she had to cut the ties not only to her mother, but in addition, she had to cut herself free from this negative conditioning. It had been so deeply imprinted that it took a long time before she felt free to act in opposition to another person's wishes. This type of control causes a totally wrong attitude to illness, either our own or someone else's.

A different pattern is observed when parents use their illness to get their own way, or as an excuse to avoid doing something they do not want to do. Since children copy or rebel according to their parents' behavior and that of older relatives and friends, they tend to adopt this method and feign illness whenever they are confronted by something they do not like or are asked to do. This, too, is a type of control.

Then there is the fear of becoming sick that is instilled into children by parents who are themselves hypochondriacs. They are given the impression that the world is a very dangerous place, full of germs and probable calamities. The children of such parentage are prone to accept this attitude, adopt it, and eventually pass it on to their own children.

Some people are health freaks who are so dedicated to the task of keeping their bodies fit that they are consumed with the urge to spend inordinate amounts of time on exercise, by working out many hours each day, which in turn can become an addiction. One woman I met is so concerned about her weight that she works out at the gym for excessively long periods every day, and is desolate if she gains a mere pound or two. Health can become a veritable fetish that controls such a person just as strongly as drugs or any other addiction.

There are also people who feel that God is punishing them when they are sick, forgetting that they themselves have caused this condition at some time in the past by word, thought, or deed, so no one can be blamed, least of all God, for their former misconduct. The present illness can be used to show them what they can learn from it now that they missed at a previous time.

Many afflictions, whether physical, mental, or emotional, frequently have their origins in the past. I have observed many instances of illness that is very incapacitating and renders the sufferer helpless in its grip. When no apparent cause has come to light in the present life, it is sometimes revealed that the person was very much into control in some way in a past life. The result of the past history is the present condition of total lack of control, even of the physical body.

Likewise, those who are now helpless under the control of another person, have undoubtedly dominated the lives of others in the past.

As Baba once informed me, I needed to learn patience, tolerance, steadfastness, and forbearance, obviously to counteract the lack of those qualities from past lives.

The biblical saying, "An eye for an eye and a tooth for a tooth" can be applied to everyone's life. Whatever we have done to others, at some time, either now or in the future, we ourselves must also experience for our own education in human values.

This work has taught me that we are not the body, but that we live in the body much the same as we live in a house. Yes, we need to keep it as clean and healthy as possible, but we don't want to be a slave to it, so that is controls us instead of our having control over it.

For example, one man told me that he received attention from his parents only when he was very sick. Only at such times did his parents show any true concern for him. Since all children crave the love and interest of their parents, they will often go to extreme limits to attract attention if they are not receiving enough.

This man was born with a tendency toward asthma and had been sickly from birth. His parents had become inured to the onset of his attacks, but they were also tired of having their life disrupted by these attacks. Between the asthma attacks, the parents would be so relieved that he was not needing them, they ignored him, obviously not wanting to make any waves when all was quiet. He quickly recognized this pattern, and when he became starved for affection, he would work himself up until he triggered a serious attack, which, from past experience, he knew would finally attract their attention.

Eventually, the attacks would occur whenever he became anxious or felt neglected. As he grew older, they happened more and more frequently. When I asked him to tell me about the attitude toward illness in his family background, he froze and was not able to recall very much. So I suggested that he ask his relatives to help him to remember anything that could be helpful. That was when he realized that he had himself unconsciously been causing his asthma attacks. The reports he received from his relatives helped him gradually to clarify the situation that originated when growing up.

I assured him that since he had unwittingly brought on the attacks, he could also consciously detach from them. This assurance made a deep impression, and he showed great enthusiasm for working with this method. For the first time he had been given hope and from then on he was excited at the prospect of taking responsibility for his own health. He willingly worked toward that end and started to practice the Figure Eight (page 92) regularly with a symbol for his old pattern in the opposite circle. He was able to visualize a symbol for his habit very easily. It was a photograph of himself as a small boy. In this photograph he could be seen looking very sad and lonely, even in the midst of his family.

CHAPTER 24

RELIGIOUS ATMOSPHERE

RELIGION IS A SUBJECT
fraught with many kinds of pressures. It can exert tremendous influence on children exposed to the more rigid aspects of various belief systems held by parents or other family members and authority figures.

One case that comes to mind involves a young man whose father was the minister of the local church. This minister cautioned his son and daughter that their behavior must always be beyond reproach or it would reflect poorly on him and his position in the community. The fear of God was instilled into them, and they grew up with the firm belief that God was like a punitive parent whom they must at all costs obey, and even fear, if they strayed too far off the narrow path outlined by their own father. They were also fully aware that their father was highly regarded by the congregation as an example of how one should live a correct life as a Christian. However, in the home they witnessed behavior quite the reverse of the father's social behavior. They observed the many times their mother, reduced to tears, was obviously in fear of his angry attacks, cruel criticism, and sarcasm. They were also fully aware that when their mother dared express an idea or made a suggestion that did not coincide with his strict code of conduct, he invariably flew into a rage. So, not only was God presented to the children as a strict and critical father figure, but their own father was a carbon copy of the image of God which he believed to be true. It was particularly confusing to the children to observe the father's very different behavior with parishioners, for with them he assumed a more benevolent attitude. The children knew that he wore a mask of sanctimonious piety when out in the parish. Who was the real person? The one with whom they lived, or the one they saw in action in public? The father's public and private personalities were very much at variance.

Some people grow up in a family in which one or both parents are professed agnostics or even atheists. In that case, the children are given little opportunity to believe in any power beyond the strictly human variety portrayed by the parents. Some of these children follow the pattern set by the parents, while others might sense an emptiness and seek to fill it in some way, even to the extent of investigating various religious practices.

In other homes, one parent may have a very strong belief while the other has none, in which case the children are confused by this contradictory message. Some may follow the example of one parent and some the other, with possibly some see-sawing back and forth between belief and disbelief. The children also react to the parents' disagreement; in which case, in their minds religion may be directly associated with quarreling and therefore is to be avoided.

Then there is the religious zealot who forces children to adhere to the same strict code that he or she chooses to espouse. Some children brought up with such parents probably rebel against any enforced rules and are turned against any type of belief as a result of this early exposure. Because each family is different, we must look back to our childhood to see the kind of atmosphere that surrounded this subject, and how our reaction to religion developed as a result.

In one family with whom I worked, both parents came from a Jewish background, the father having been born in Poland and the mother in the United States. The father had run away from home at age 12 when he learned that he, along with other young boys his age, would be conscripted into the army. He had experienced what it was like to be born a Jew, so despite the fact that he was the firstborn son, destined to carry the inherited role of cohan or teacher in the temple, he turned away from his Jewish heritage and discarded all the accoutrements when he left the country as a stowaway on a ship bound for the United States. He remained without any belief from then on, married, had three children, and lived a very successful and social life. His children were reared in that atmosphere even though their mother tried to have them attend synagogue with her, as she had followed her parents who were staunchly faithful to their inherited beliefs.

Suddenly, the father discovered Mary Baker Eddy and converted to Christian Science, pored over her written words, and followed her teachings. The effect on the children was confusing and the change in their family life was quite extreme. Replacing the social and materialistic father who enjoyed the luxuries of life and who had encouraged them to follow in his footsteps, was a father who suddenly swung in the opposite direction and expected them to follow suit. To them religion changed their lives and their father, and they blamed it for the abrupt change. From then on, whenever they were sick, they were not allowed to see a doctor. Instead, a Christian Science practitioner was called to treat them. The pool table they had in the home was relegated to the basement and never again used. In fact, life became very drab and overly serious, and lacking in any type of enjoyment. The result was that the children turned away from any kind of religious belief and reared their own children in a similar way.

Then there are the families in which the parents come from different backgrounds, inherited belief systems, and often from very different national roots. It is hard enough for two people to make the necessary adjustment to one another when they marry or decide to live together. But when there are also seemingly insurmountable differences in family background, the adjustment is even more difficult for each of them to make, and frequently repeated quarreling is the result.

The effect of the mixed heritage on the children of such a union poses another kind of problem, especially after the children start school and mix with other children, most of whom will not have the same background. In addition, there is often hostility coming from various members of the two families, for everyone has a personal opinion based on a particular heritage. Since the religious teachings usually dictate the way many families choose to conduct their life, the children are imprinted at an early age with the particular religious teachings to which their parents adhere. This, in turn, tends to determine how they will raise their own children later.

Because this early conditioning takes place on a subconscious level, those who follow the dictates set forth by the parents' choice of a religious expression automatically either follow or rebel against it.

Therefore, whatever the climate happens to have been in our family, it needs, first, to be made conscious by looking back to discover the particular pattern it took. A symbol to represent the pattern has to be found, and placed in the opposite circle of the Figure Eight (page 92) for the usual two weeks of practice. It can then be released. Its control over us is no longer in effect in our life after we cut apart the two circles to detach ourselves from the old pattern.

Then we are free to decide just what we can believe, as well as how we can implement our beliefs into our daily life. In this way, we will have assumed responsibility for our conduct instead of continuing to be controlled by other people's beliefs. Automatically accepting religion—or turning against it—does not allow us to have a spiritual center that originates from our hearts. This is something we each may want to look into when we examine our patchwork quilt.

CHAPTER 25

SEXUAL ATTITUDES

THE SUBJECT OF SEX varies enormously in various cultures. In some countries it is discussed openly, and the taboos and practices are presented without embarrassment. Where this is the case, young people grow up without forbidden ideas about sex, and accept it as a part of life, but not, however, the most important part, as is so often believed when the subject is kept under cover. But in many countries it is never discussed, which results in confusion, particularly for the young. Interestingly enough, in India, where such books as the Kama Sutra and volumes on Tantric Yoga originated, it is not considered proper to talk about sex or to mention the sexual organs. In direct contrast, in some of the South Sea Island cultures, where the old practices are still observed, the young boys and girls at the age of puberty are removed from their parents' dwelling for a specific time and occupy communal houses, one for the boys and one for the girls. The elders, or wise men and women of the tribe, instruct them about the duties and customs of the group that have been handed down for many generations. These instructions include teaching young people about sex and choosing a partner.

When the sexual part of life is kept secret, suppressed thoughts and fantasies flourish, and often erupt in compulsive behavior when aroused and stimulated in many different ways, particularly by the media. In many parts of the world, including the USA, the pendulum has swung in the opposite direction, and the result is that an exaggerated importance has been placed on sexuality. All kinds of sex is portrayed on television, in movies and plays, and now the latest venue is the Internet, where anyone can watch and listen to myriad variations on the subject. Small children are confronted with visual and graphic demonstrations of a wide variety of sexual practices. This material is beyond their understanding so they have no way to process it. It goes directly into the subconscious and can erupt in later life, causing serious and often extremely embarrassing problems.

In addition to these more general and extensive influences, the parents' beliefs and practices have a profound effect on the offspring. Children are quick to sense disparities between what parents say and what they actually do. This, of course, also applies to a wide range of topics, but it is especially important with regard to sex. If one or both of the parents instruct children that extramarital sex is taboo, yet the children are aware, or suspect that their parents' behavior belies that advice, the children are being given mixed messages. If, on the other hand, a parent is overly puritanical and sets hard and fast rules for the children, this can cause rebellion and a determination to flout such rigid demands.

Since we cannot change or teach our parents, we must find a symbol that represents their attitude to sex and cut away from it to remove the overlay of their beliefs that we carry, so that we can find out what is applicable for us.

The subject of incest and sexual abuse also has to be considered. It is far more prevalent than has been apparent in the past because it has remained hidden in most cultures. Children who have suffered from any form of sexual abuse, especially from a parent, sibling, close relative, minister, priest, or teacher have usually been warned by the abuser of the dire consequences if they dare to mention it to anyone. These threats ensure that the abuse is kept secret. Fortunately, such problems are starting to surface so they can be dealt with openly. Incest has a devastating effect on a child and continues to produce feelings of unworthiness and defilement that lead to many diverse problems in later life, particularly involving dating and eventually finding a mate.

Unfortunately, a healthy and sane, or practical attitude toward sex seems to be fairly rare because of the way information is passed from one generation to the next. It is essential to cut the ties to whatever attitudes parents inherited and to which we have, as their children, been exposed. This exercise can free us to discover what is correct for us, which may not necessarily be what our parents have passed on to us. Opening to our own sexuality may not be a way of life that is approved of by our parents.

It is, therefore, not always sufficient to cut the ties to the parents. If the atmosphere around the subject of sex has been strongly imprinted, the thought form must also be released. This is particularly true in cases of incest, where the entire subject has been sullied and connected in the child's mind with fear, guilt, and often self-loathing.

Finding a symbol to represent the family attitude toward sex, and visualizing it in the Figure Eight for two weeks, followed by the usual cuttings and destruction of the symbol, will help to free you from family control. Then you can ascertain your own attitude about sex.

CHAPTER 26

ROLES IN MARRIAGE AND PARTNERSHIP

THE TRADITIONS THAT have grown up around the role of man and woman, and the relationship between the two, play a crucial part in the future attitude of the growing child. Some of these traditions are valid, while others are outmoded, because of the many dramatic changes that have occurred in the world during a relatively short period of time. With changes in family structure, an equal change must also take place regarding the concept of partnership between men and women in all aspects of daily life, whether in the home, socially, in the world, or in the workplace.

Many members of both sexes have been reared to believe that women do not need higher education, and that if they do attend college, their goal should be to find a husband to support them together with any children they may eventually have. This belief is so deep seated that many women are paralyzed by it, often without any conscious awareness of its affect on their lives. They absorbed these family beliefs to such an extent that these beliefs have become part of their very being. In other words, the beliefs are often so strong they control the family members who adhere rigidly to the old ways.

Men have been programmed by a similar belief, with the result that many men refuse to allow their wives to work outside the home. They act as if it is a slight to themselves if their wives work. They think that it implies they are not capable of supporting the family and need the additional financial help of the wife.

Until such old out-moded patterns are released, both partners are trapped by them, and they are not free to achieve their potential. The old patterns cause resentment, especially if women are forced by circumstances to work outside the home when they were taught that their role should really be that of a housewife and mother.

Another behavior pattern was brought to my attention recently. A married couple had reversed the usual roles of husband and wife. The wife was the breadwinner, out in the world earning a living, while the husband minded the home and children; he marketed, cooked the meals, and cleaned the house. When I inquired into their childhood and family backgrounds, the origin of these reversed patterns became clear. The husband had been reared in a home where his father had died when he and his siblings were still quite small, leaving their mother the dual task of being the wage earner and the homemaker. This was a situation she did not choose; it was thrust upon her by the circumstances in which she was left after her husband's death.

It had a most interesting effect upon her two sons. One had married a very competent woman who successfully ran her own business, a job that kept her away from home all day except for weekends and holidays. They had two children and after the birth of each, she had arranged to stay home for a short period of time, but continued to supervise her business from the home. The care of the house, garden, and children fell onto the husband's shoulders, even though he, too, held down a job, though, in his case, it could be accomplished from home.

The other brother reacted to the early childhood situation of being the child of a single parent, in this case, the mother, in a very different way from his brother. He, too, married and fathered two children. But, unlike his brother, he forbade his wife to work. He was adamant in his attitude, even though his wife was a college graduate and was most unhappy not to be allowed to continue with the career she had pursued before marriage. It was obvious that this son rebelled against the situation he observed regarding his mother, and he wanted to make sure his children had the undivided attention of their mother, which he always craved while he was growing up.

Each brother criticized the other's lifestyle, failing to see that they both reacted to the conditions prevailing in their home life as children, but in opposite ways. Neither reaction is right or wrong; they are just different. They both locked into the role they had unconsciously elected to assume as they observed and reacted to the family pattern. They felt deprived because they had no father, and their mother was too occupied with her work to give them sufficient attention to meet their individual needs.

Another family pattern that had a critical effect on the children involved a family consisting of parents and two children. The father worked outside the home, but his income was not sufficient to meet the ever-increasing needs of the family. To augment his income, the mother took a job against her wishes. She constantly complained that she could not give her children the attention they needed, and blamed this situation on the fact that she had to work. In this case, in the eyes of the children, work was considered a thief that stole from them the attention they craved from their mother. Consequently, they developed an attitude about work that resulted in work being considered an evil necessity. However, at the same time, they observed that their mother thrived on the recognition and success she received at work, so their aim was to achieve the praise and financial gain they saw that their mother relished, instead of seeing work as service. Work became, in their eyes, a necessary burden that could be alleviated only if it brought with it acclaim for the effort they expended, and the remuneration they received was overly important. Such mixed messages are confusing to children faced with the task of finding their own future patterns regarding work. This confusion persists unless they cut the ties to the original attitude that programmed them as children.

Looked upon from the standpoint of the patchwork quilt, these roles could provide the means whereby much needed learning could take place.

This brings up the age-old question concerning the traditional roles of men and women when interacting, whether in the home, socially, or in the workplace. The outdated concept that men are superior to women in every way has been proved to be erroneous. Many women have undertaken jobs that once were traditionally held by men and have proved that they are, in most cases, extremely capable and successful in fulfilling them. The long history of male dominance appears to be coming to an end now that both men and women are gainfully employed in so many previously male-dominated institutions.

We have to bear in mind that at the Hi C level we are all equal in value, which means we must live as if this were true rather than just mouth it. We must act in a way that supports the concept.

Each partner is an individual who has certain abilities to contribute to the partnership, if given an opportunity to do so freely and without control by the other partner. The husband is not necessarily always right in his views and preferences, but neither is the woman. Only when each defers to the Hi C can they hope to surmount differences and difficulties and live more harmoniously together, with mutual respect for each other.

The children of a harmonious partnership will be most fortunate in being exposed to positive role models for their future lives. However, this change from the old ways requires better communication skills between couples, which are woefully lacking in the world and especially between the sexes. Both partners must learn to listen to the other instead of primarily talking, and even when speaking, each should be aware when the other needs to interrupt if he or she has something pertinent to say that will enhance the exchange between them. Children learn by imitation of the parents' example, and grow up with the same beliefs.

New attitudes more fitting to the present time in our world cycle must be adopted in order to avoid disagreement and tension between partners. Only by cutting the ties to the old atmosphere can new concepts be developed. After cutting the ties (page 92), it is essential that the Maypole be used (pages 9 and 146), so each partner can put aside his or her personal opinion to seek the direction of the Hi C. Only in this way can harmony be preserved so that both egos are no longer battling for control of either the situation or each other.

When two people are willing to put aside their personal opinions or wishes, and seek the direction of the Hi C, harmony can be preserved. When a family is willing to practice the Maypole Exercise on a regular basis, with each of the members seeking direction from the Hi C, life becomes much easier, with fewer battles of wills, and less manipulation exerted by various family members.

The Family Maypole is an excellent way to link up all the members of a family or group to the joint Hi C, which raises the consciousness of everyone and ensures the guidance of the Hi C instead of the ego of any one in the group. Use the Maypole Exercise (on page 9) and the variation below to heal the family.

EXERCISE 5
THE FAMILY MAYPOLE

To set up the Maypole for family use, imagine it in the middle of the room with many different colored ribbons attached to the top and hanging down all around it. The top of the Maypole represents the Hi C for each person.

Imagine you are walking up to the Maypole and choosing the colored ribbon that appeals to you. Holding the ribbon in your hand, imagine you are returning to your seat connected to the Hi C by your ribbon. If you wish, you can ask for a symbol of the Hi C to appear at the top of the Maypole to make it more real for you.

Observe how each member in the group is forming a triangle with everyone else in the room, with the help of the ribbons. The ribbon can be like a telephone connection between each person and the Hi C.

Ask the Hi C to give you, via your ribbon, whatever you need and are ready to accept. Let your palms be open in your lap like little bowls ready to receive whatever is forthcoming.

Breathe in what is being given you and thank the Hi C for the answer to your request. Breathe out any doubts you may have that could block your receptivity.

If you are lucky enough to have a family or a group to work with, this is a nice group meditation, and can help solve a number of problems or differences in the family or the group.

CHAPTER 27

CHILDBIRTH

THE SUBJECT OF CHILD-
birth is fraught with fear and superstition that exerts a
strong influence on women who face the possibility of bear-
ing a child. Many old wives tales are alive and flourishing in
many present-day cultures. Some of these stories have been
handed down from generation to generation, and are ad-
hered to despite the fact that they are not valid in our current society.

Young girls grow up with the belief that childbirth has to
be painful, and can even cost them their life, even though
they have received an education that refutes these beliefs.
Such beliefs have been accepted by the subconscious where
they remain unless (and until) they are released. Many
women carry their fears throughout pregnancy and then
wonder why their baby is born with fear, which is expressed
by colic, extreme shyness, intense rebellion, prolonged cry-
ing spells, or some other symptom that is equally disturbing
to the parents.

There is also the pressure caused by a preference for a child of the acceptable sex, which is often exerted in families where a male heir is important.

Many midwives and doctors who have guided the prospective mothers through the cutting of the ties to their own mother have reported that when this is done, the pregnancy and eventual birth are greatly eased. In addition, if a pregnant woman also cuts the ties to the attitude or beliefs held by the family members, it will free her to be able to discard those negative beliefs and customs that have been attached to what should be a natural and rewarding experience. Fortunately, there is a great deal of material readily available to young parents to help them approach the birth of their child with a positive attitude. With so much help available, and with the possibility of releasing outmoded concepts, fears, and superstitions, the whole experience connected to childbirth can be a relaxed and happy one.

When this is the case, the baby born in such a setting will most likely be free from any fear picked up from the mother. The result is that the child will be happier and healthier and easier to raise. There are many old ideas and concepts that still remain in certain families. These old beliefs will no longer affect the birth now that future parents can attend groups designed to acquaint them with the very latest practices attendant on pregnancy and childbirth. One outmoded concept is that the expectant mother must limit her activities in various ways to protect the developing fetus. This subject is most confusing, as there are many conflicting directives that can cause anxiety. In my own case, my mother had repeatedly recounted to me the direful events surrounding my birth. She would regale me with the details of the three days of labor pains she was forced

to endure before I was delivered, always ending the oft repeated saga with the fact that my entry into the world had
almost caused her death. This tale of woe ill-prepared me
to face having children of my own. However, as I was an
only child, I had always had a strong desire to have more
than one child, which may to some extent have offset the
fear that my mother managed to instill in me during the
impressionable years while I was growing up under her
control.

With my first child, a daughter, I was given conventional
care and preparation, with an anaesthetic to dull the labor
pains. But this method caused me to be unconscious when
my baby was delivered, and in addition, I literally escaped
from the pain, and along with it, I also escaped from the
fears that my mother had programmed in. With my second
pregnancy, I decided I would be fully conscious so I could
welcome my baby as soon as he or she was born. No drugs
were administered, and I was among the first to experience
the natural childbirth method which was only just being introduced in this country at that time. My doctor was willing
to teach me how to relax at the onset of labor pains, using
deep breathing to aid the process. During the actual labor,
I quickly discovered that if I could follow his instructions at
the very onset of each contraction, I was able to flow with it
instead of resisting the process. The result was a delivery,
though not entirely free from pain, that was certainly within
bearable limits. The most gratifying aspect was being a part
of the process. I was able to do my part to bring my daughter into the world in as natural a way as possible. As I look
back, I realize that perhaps the true gift was to see my
daughter as soon as she emerged, and before the umbilical
cord was severed.

This experience also taught me an invaluable lesson that has been an enormous help in dealing with everyday stress from the pressures of life. I discovered that fatigue is closely linked to resistance. If we resist anything, we become tense and rigid, which in turn blocks the flow of energy throughout the entire body, and we become tired from this lack of energy.

CHAPTER 28

PARENTING

I REMEMBER HEARING "Spare the rod and spoil the child" repeated many times during my childhood. At that time it seemed to be too harsh, but since then the pendulum has swung to an extreme in the opposite direction, from the overly strict discipline during my youth, to the present permissive situation observable in many parts of the world.

We all might want to look back at the way we were brought up, to determine whether we have repeated the manner in which we were raised, or if we have gone in the opposite direction when raising our own children.

As I look back, I recall the way my strict and dominating mother expected me not to be seen and certainly not to be heard. I was soundly beaten if I as much as dared to assert myself or if I even inquired about what I had done wrong. My mother was one of eleven children born to a mother who became deaf as a result of scarlet fever. The eldest daughter had to assume her role, and so resented it that she was overly strict and repressive with her younger siblings.

My mother apparently rebelled violently against such restrictive treatment, and broke away from the family as soon as possible by taking a job, which in those days was unusual for a woman of that class. My father came from a very different family pattern. He was one of five children born to parents who were much more lenient. I was the only child, so my mother justified her harsh treatment of me by explaining that she was not going to bring up a spoiled brat like many "only" children turned out to be. I doubt that she was ever aware of the fact that she was repeating the same treatment she received as a child at the hands of her older sister, though in an even more domineering and punitive manner.

My father was in the middle of two brothers and two sisters. His father was a gentleman farmer with many farms under his supervision. So life was less stressful for him than it was for most families. The atmosphere in which the children were raised was much less strict. Consequently, my mother was mortally afraid that my father would spoil me, given a chance, so she did everything in her power to prevent that from happening.

When I married I vowed never to repeat the kind of treatment I had suffered at her hands if I had children. But when I did become a mother I soon discovered that it would be equally wrong to bend over backward to overindulge my children, so I was forced to seek a middle path—neither too strict nor too lenient. My husband had a strict and punitive father, and a mother who spoiled him because he was the firstborn son in a Jewish family. So the two differing patterns we each brought with us into the marriage had to be reconciled.

My mother always insisted that I do exactly what she wanted. She was convinced her way was not only right, but it was the only way. So I was given no choice but to follow the path she outlined for me. Had I rebelled, the immediate punishment I knew from experience would be far too painful and damaging to risk. Given this extreme treatment, I was careful to encourage my daughters to find their own way in choosing a career, though I was willing to give them advice whenever they sought my help. I am sure I made many mistakes, albeit, unconsciously, as we all do, but of one point I was certain. In the reverie work I had been taught that far too often parents project on their children what they think the children should be and do, instead of trying to find out what each child has within it to be expressed. It became obvious to me that the widespread educational methods in effect in most parts of the world must eventually change to free the youth to bring about the very necessary and urgently needed changes that will ensure the survival of our present civilization.

Many children tell me they want real people as their mother and father, and not the roles their parents assume in their work situation, which does not belong in the home. Parents would do well to make it a habit to practice the Figure Eight with a symbol for their work role when they leave their workplace to go home, so that they can detach temporarily from the work role and are free to assume the role of husband, wife, and caring parent. Then children will feel validated as acceptable and worthwhile members of the family, which is essential for them if they are to succeed in adjusting to the rapidly changing conditions in the world. In this way, and only then, will they have the necessary confidence to initiate essential changes in the environment and in society. In addition, youth of both sexes can undergo cutting parental ties upon attaining puberty. The wise ancient cultures were aware that this was a most important step in the development of the members of the next generation.

Though it may seem strange, I have observed that parents treat their own children in the same way as they themselves were treated, even when that treatment was strict or even cruel. I learned this when I worked with families in which one or both parents had been in a Nazi prison camp. One might expect that having been treated so cruelly and heartlessly that these people would vow never to repeat that behavior with children and would treat them very differently. But such is not always the case. In some cases the abused adults are as harsh with their children as their jailors were with them.

CHAPTER 29

SKELETONS IN THE CLOSET

In many families there is a hidden event that is never discussed. However, children have an uncanny ability to sense these forbidden topics. They tune in to them on the subconscious level, but because they are not available to the conscious mind, they are not able to process them, so they remain unknown, haunting them, and causing a vague feeling of unrest, or even guilt—and sometimes a sense of unworthiness.

There are many different events that can affect children in this way. For instance, if a child is illegitimate, born out of wedlock, a bastard, it will have an uneasy feeling about itself for no known reason. In such cases, it is most important to discuss this issue with the child as soon as he or she is old enough to understand, which varies with each child. If this has not been done by the time the child reaches puberty, it is not too late to cut the ties to the underlying atmosphere built up around such a birth, as well as providing a simple explanation geared to the child's level of understanding. If an abortion was attempted, but failed, this too, can remain in the subconscious as a traumatic memory. This memory can result in a strong sense of rejection despite the fact that the parents have tried to make up to the child in an effort to compensate in some way for the original rejection, or may even spoil and overindulge the child. This treatment often causes confusion due to the fact that the original rejection is still very much alive at the subconscious level. Again, it is invariably helpful to explain the circumstances surrounding the birth at the appropriate time, together with the reassurance that the child is very welcome and loved.

In a family where there has been a miscarriage or abortion, it is preferable to discuss it at some point with the older children in the family.

In some families other types of events may have occurred that have remained hidden because of shame or fear of the results should they be made known. One of these is death, especially of a parent by suicide, murder, or some means other than a normal death. Imprisonment is often an embarrassment to the family members of the prisoner, and should be explained in simple terms to the children involved.

If one thinks that adoption is a matter of secrecy, there is another family secret that is even more hidden. It happens when a family takes on a relative or a stranger who is not adopted, but who is raised as a family member with other children. In one family, a young girl, the child of a young woman who was raped, was given to a distant relative to be raised with the family. No formal adoption papers were signed. This girl did not look like her "sisters"—even remotely. It wasn't until she was on her deathbed that she learned who she was. She had spent her life looking for something, but did not know what it was, and this longing created a great depression. Evidently several people in the family knew the story, but no one talked about it.

Another often undiscussed fact involves the original parentage of an adopted child. Adopted children frequently carry a sense of being different from their peers and often have an unconscious, yet persistent yearning for something lost. The adoptive parents usually prefer that the child they chose to adopt consider them to be the parents and will deliberately keep from the child the actual facts of its birth. But the child may develop different characteristics from the adoptive parents and then feel that he or she does not belong in that family. It is, therefore, important to tell the child, as soon as possible, of its original heritage. At the same time, it is also important to let the child know that he or she was very much wanted, and received a warm welcome from the adoptive parents, perhaps even more so than some children who were not adopted. This reassurance is absolutely essential to ensure that the child will be given an antidote to what he or she may perceive as rejection at birth. But even with such careful preparation, at the subconscious level the child will still be fully aware of this original rejection, and will want to cut the ties with both sets of parents after attaining puberty. It is especially important to ask the Hi C to forgive the child's original parents for giving the child up for adoption.

CHAPTER 30

PLAYFULNESS AND FUN

ONE YOUNG MAN TOLD me that he recently became aware that he felt guilty whenever he was doing something he enjoyed, or when he was having a good time and was feeling happy. As we discussed his situation, it became clear that this pattern originated in childhood. His father had insisted that all the children should be taught to work hard. In fact he placed hard work above all other activities. If he caught any of his children idling or wasting time, which included doing anything that was not work related, he would immediately give them some task to execute. At the same time, he delivered a lecture on the dangers of wasting time. The children reacted by engaging in pleasurable pursuits in secret, but they were constantly in fear of being found out and punished.

Before this particular session, I had often wondered how I might help this young man to lighten up, as he was always so deadly serious, and never seemed able to relax and have any fun. I had also noticed that he rarely laughed or even smiled, so I was not at all sure that he even possessed a sense of humor.

In this particular case, a work ethic was handed down from one generation to the next. This man was the first one in the family line who was willing to do something to break the chain reaction, primarily because it was causing him such extreme anxiety and discomfort. After he cut the ties to the symbol that represented this attitude, he was able to make changes in his lifestyle that left room for play. I suggested that he repeat from time to time the little nursery rhyme, "All work and no play makes Jack a dull boy."

My own childhood offers another example of the mistaken belief that it's wrong to enjoy life and have fun or be playful. My mother had her own ideas regarding how I should be trained. In her case, it did not so much stem from her inherited or acquired concepts. It was more important that she be the beneficiary while I was allotted the role of provider of the benefits. From an early age I was expected to take over many of the household tasks she disliked, for she was not temperamentally suited to the role of housewife or mother.

I quickly recognized this pattern. I also discovered that the only way I could avoid having to do whatever she had in mind was to be engaged in school work. Education was important in her opinion, and therefore my academic success would reflect on her as a good mother. The result was that I became a veritable bookworm, and she would frequently comment that I "always had my nose in a book." It is obvious that I did not have an opportunity to learn how to play or have fun like other children, for I was far too serious and withdrawn. Thanks to this work, I cut the ties to that old role which allowed me to become lighter in my outlook and face each day with less solemnity and more lightheartedness.

Then there are those people who are on a so-called spiritual path and mistakenly equate spirituality with deadly seriousness. But this gives a totally erroneous impression and could never attract many people to become interested in their belief. In such cases, instead of allowing the Hi C to shine through their outer personality, their own will and ego are getting in the way and preventing the Hi C from expressing Itself through them.

We should be able to alternate between seriousness when that is appropriate, and a more lighthearted approach when that is called for. Unfortunately, the joy is missing in some groups engaged in spiritual practice. Many people equate spirituality with an assumed and studied seriousness and a "holier than thou" attitude. They disapprove of any form of enjoyment, deeming frivolity as the work of the Devil.

Children raised in a home where one or both parents presented this example will either conform to this rigid regime, or, as soon as they leave home, they will rebel, often going to the opposite extreme in an attempt to overcome the early restrictions. But neither of these reactions, copying or rebelling, necessarily represents the type of behavior that is correct for them, or, for that matter, for the current situation in the culture into which they were born.

This does not mean that we should be joking all day or making fun of others, or merely being frivolous. Rather, it implies keeping a light touch, and retaining an optimistic view, instead of exhibiting a long face and solemn manner. To achieve this lighter attitude is indeed a challenge, especially when problems seem to crop up and demand immediate attention at a vastly increased rate.

The secret is to try to remain centered, and to retain an attitude of detachment, so we can accept whatever happens, whether we like it or not. Only in this way can we remain relaxed and light. As in the Black and White Bird Exercise that follows, refrain from either pushing away the things we don't like or grabbing those we want.

EXERCISE 6
BLACK AND WHITE BIRDS BALANCE OPPOSITES

This exercise helps to initiate an attitude of acceptance of all pairs of opposites, such as good and bad, happy and unhappy, pain and pleasure, praise and blame, to name but a few. Imagine you are walking a tightrope, carefully placing one foot in front of the other, looking straight ahead, with arms stretched out to each side, with palms facing up.

Imagine a big black bird over on your left side. You fear it may attack you. Resist the impulse to push it away, which would cause you to fall off the tightrope.

Continue to walk ahead, looking neither to the right nor to the left. Imagine a beautiful gleaming white bird over on your right side. Resist the desire to reach out to take hold of it, which would again cause you to fall off the tightrope.

Continue your way across the tightrope, allowing either the black or the white bird to alight on your up-turned palm whenever it wishes.

This exercise results in an attitude of acceptance of whatever life brings onto your path, which leads to peace. Practice this technique at least once a day for the best results, whenever you believe that you need it.

CHAPTER 31

PREJUDICE AS A
FAMILY PATTERN

IN MANY FAMILIES
deep-seated prejudices have been imprinted on the members. Many national groups hold the firm conviction that they are vastly superior to those of other nations. So strong is this belief that people often forbid their children to associate with other nationalities. Intermarriage between a family member and someone from a different national heritage is taboo, and parents will go to great lengths to prevent their children from what they consider would be a disaster if the young people should defy this taboo. To a large extent, this situation is becoming less common as more young people meet students from other countries in school and college, and go against these outmoded traditions to form alliances with partners their parents would deem unsuitable.

But prejudice still rears its ugly head in other areas. It stems from the mistaken belief that certain nationalities, and therefore the individuals comprising them, are, in some way, superior to those of other groups. This very concept is a fallacy, according to the teaching I have been given in my work. At the level of the Real Self or Hi C, all beings are of equal value. No one is better than or worse than any other. Only the personality and lifestyle are different, not the main seed or spark. So, to teach the young that because they were born into a certain national group or race they are automatically special, or chosen of God, is the ultimate lie. Along similar lines, it is far from the truth to teach children that if they have been born to a family that is considered important or influential in the community where they live, that they are better than people born in less successful or affluent circumstances.

The craving to be considered better than others causes severe problems, both in individuals and in nations. In the latter case, it is one of the main causes of wars between nations or opposing factions within a country, as in Ireland, Korea, Serbia, and so on. This erroneous belief causes bloodshed, starvation, and homelessness to countless people who have been allowed no voice in the decision to wage war, but are caught, as in a trap, due to the decisions of their respective governments.

So, we need to check the atmosphere in our family relating to any kind of prejudice or feeling of superiority over another person or group. The reverse also needs to be considered. Were we made to feel less worthy than others?

In some families a reverse snobbery is evident. The children are given to understand that they are, for some reason, of less value, or less important than other children. I remember a saying that was common while I was growing up in England that summed up this sentiment in a clear and interesting way. It was, "Don't try to be too big for your boots." Another oft-repeated but equally damaging comment was, "Who do you think you are?" implying the same message, that the person being thus addressed was inferior in some way to others.

The reasons usually given for this kind of belief are numerous. It may be because of race, color, nationality, religious affiliation, age, gender, personal appearance, parents' occupation, parents' social position, how much money earned, and many other reasons. This type of programming can either spur people to succeed at all costs in a valiant effort to prove their validity and defy the stigma placed upon them, or they believe what they have been told and live in the shadow of this very low image with no prospect of overcoming it.

In either case, early conditioning controls the person. However, as we have seen in many other cases of control from outer sources, it can be neutralized by practicing the Figure Eight for the usual two weeks with a symbol representing the offensive message in the other circle and then detaching from its control by separating the two circles and destroying the symbol representing the control factor.

I have seen many cases where this has been most successful, especially when the Hour Glass Exercise is practiced at the same time.

EXERCISE 7
THE HOUR GLASS

The Hour glass is a symbol to aid in removing the ceiling many people either place, or have had placed, over their lives, which limits them in many ways.

To use the Hour Glass, visualize a golden circle at arm's length all around you on the ground. Imagine you are pulling it up around you in the shape of a golden cone, with the point or top slightly above your head. Erect another inverted cone above the first one, with the two points meeting at the neck of the hour glass with the Hi C at that site.

Visualize the upper cone wide open to the sky. Ask the Hi C to bring whatever It knows you need from anywhere in the universe into the upper cone, so that it can then filter down into your life at the appropriate time and rate. If you have a specific need or request, ask that the solution or answer be brought to you in this way, but try not to be too specific about what you want to receive. Let the Hi C decide for you.

Thank the Hi C for whatever it will send you, surrender to Its will, promise to trust It to bring you what only It knows you need. Vow to accept whatever It sends you, whether you approve or not.

It also has to be remembered that all the evaluations that have been projected on us are all connected to the body (or physical aspects) and we have been shown that we should not identify with the body/mind/personality, but with whom we really are (our true identity), which is the Hi C, at which level we are all equal in value.

So, whether we have been taught that we are very special and the chosen of God, or the opposite, that we are less than others, if either of these ideologies has controlled us, we can remind ourselves that we are not helpless under its influence. We have been given the means whereby we can detach from this overlay and become free to express our Real Selves by cutting the ties that connect us to it.

CHAPTER 32

POSSESSIONS

There is a current trend for people to judge their own value, as well as that of others, by possessions. The so-called status symbols include houses, cars, clothes, jewels, and the myriad articles that money can procure. In social gatherings it is not unusual to observe guests carefully checking the clothes, shoes, watches, jewelry, and even the eye glasses of other guests to determine whether they are of the very latest design and if the owners of these possessions are worth getting to know. They don't make that decision on the actual people, themselves, but on the articles that others use to adorn themselves. The same scrutiny is applied to the house and furnishings, and the cars in the garage, if the gathering takes place in the host's home.

Children brought up in a family where surface values are accepted and practiced will react in one of two different ways. Either they will adopt them and repeat the same attitude as the parents and cultivate friends only if they fall into the category of owning the latest, most expensive, and therefore the most sought after possessions. They also evaluate other children in the same way they see their parents choose friends and acquaintances—by possessions, and not by their character.

Sometimes the children rebel and are likely to veer off in the opposite direction. They scorn the objects that money can buy and deliberately choose friends who come from a very different background, much to their parents' consternation. Others may take the so-called "spiritual" approach that decrees that possessions are superfluous and pose a threat to their spiritual path, and so must be avoided at any cost.

These attitudes are merely reactions to whatever has been encountered in the family, so they do not necessarily represent true values for each person. We all can look back into our childhood to see our family's attitude to belongings. What kind of a background did each of our parents come from and how did they react to it in a way that has affected us? Our parents may have been raised in families with similar values or with very different ones. In the latter case, we probably have grown up with mixed messages that caused confusion around the subject of evaluating other people. Whatever the climate happened to be, we can find a symbol that represents it, and practice the Figure Eight (page 92) for at least two weeks with the symbol in the opposite circle from our own. Then cut the ties to this controlling pattern. This will free us to determine the values we will choose to live by. As soon as we make this decision, our relationships with other people will undergo a radical change for the better. We will no longer be tempted to judge others by outer appearances or possessions, but by what they are really like as human beings. Eventually we will be able to see beyond or behind the personality and catch a glimpse of the Hi C residing within the outer covering. At that level, all are equal in value, none either more or less worthy than anyone else. When this point is finally reached, all others will be accepted as members of the world family with everyone being a sister or a brother.

At such point in time, when more and more people are arriving at this stage in their development, the world will become a more peaceful, loving, and less stressful place in which to live. That state can be likened to the Golden Age that has been predicted by the ancient seers and prophets. So, we have a choice, either to be part of the problem or part of the cure. With that knowledge clearly in mind, we will begin to realize how useless it is to continue to be critical of the world situation. We can decide to accept the fact that we have been a part of it by contributing to the wrong approach. This realization can free us to be more directly in touch with the HI C and to dedicate our lives to becoming Its instruments instead of continuing to be slaves to our egos and desires, or remaining unaware of our true identity as part of—and therefore no different from—the overall God.

CHAPTER 33

CLOTHES AND FASHION

From ancient times, clothes have been an important part of people's lives. Originally they were strictly utilitarian, to protect the body from harm or the vicissitudes of the climate. Early tribespeople must have envied the animals and birds their fur, skin, and feathers, so when they killed to provide themselves with food, they converted the skins into coverings for their naked bodies. In time, they began to add various kinds of decoration to make the skins more attractive. The women eventually began to weave fabric from natural materials and started to make clothing. Clothing made from fabric was much more convenient and comfortable during warmer times of the year. Gradually, more creative energy was expended as women began to compete with one another to produce intricate patterns and designs for clothing. Other women who were less creative would copy the new designs, and in this way fashions began to emerge and have continued for centuries all over the world.

In different countries the style of clothing was adapted to the climate of the area, so apparel in tropical climates was very different from that worn in colder areas. Some of these original types of clothing, such as saris for women and dhotis for men in India are still being worn. But many people are discarding traditional national dress in preference for a worldwide uniform borrowed from the American jeans and t-shirts look popular with young men and women.

As these drastic changes are taking place after centuries of very few changes, a big adjustment is required, particularly on the part of the older generation. Many young men and women think it is absolutely essential to wear the very latest fashions in order to fit in with their peer group. This trend leads them to identify others with the clothes they wear and to judge them accordingly, which is obviously a most limited attitude. "Clothes do not make the man," is a saying that was popular when I was growing up at the beginning of the past century. Many affluent men and women even chose to wear old and shabby garments as a badge of disdain for those who blindly followed the dictates of fashion.

So, as with other attitudes around the many various subjects, we each must look back to determine the family attitude toward clothes and fashion, and how our parents adjusted to the abrupt changes taking place in their children's lives.

Were our lives made miserable by being forced to wear clothes that our parents considered suitable, but which were so different from the clothes other children were wearing that we felt we did not fit in with our peers? I distinctly recall being made to wear a very beautiful embroidered silk dress given to me by one of my aunts. None of the other children wore anything like this, so I felt "different" and was miserable.

Or, we may have been born into a low income family and had to wear clothes that were too small or too large because they were handed down from older brothers or sisters. Or we were sent to school dressed as fashion plates and were afraid to soil the expensive clothes our parents dictated we should wear. Whatever our experience happened to be, we now can ask if the early conditioning is still controlling us, in which case, we can cut the ties to it so we can decide what is appropriate for us at the present time, now that we are no longer children under the care of our parents.

We are not the body, but nor should we identify with the clothes we wear. However, clothing should reflect our station in life and be suitable for our occupation. Above all, our clothes should reflect our personality so that we feel at ease in them and therefore do not need to give them a thought after we have dressed for an occasion. In other words, clothes should not be allowed to distract us or occupy our mind to the exclusion of other far more important topics.

Jewels and hairstyles must be included in this category, for they, too, should not control us, nor should we equate our own worth with the adornments we choose to wear, for neither they nor the body on which we wear them should control us or affect our evaluation of ourselves in any way.

I have seen instances where friends and relatives of a newly engaged couple scrutinize the ring the young woman is wearing and judge the poor man who gave it to her according to the estimated cost of the stone.

Another fairly recent trend is to copy the clothes or hairstyle of celebrities, such as movie stars. In so doing, women all over the world seek to emulate these role models and in some unknown way, hope to have the stars' charisma wipe off on themselves. Princess Diana was the focus for many women who wore inexpensive copies of her clothes and copied her hairstyle to make themselves look like she did.

Many of these conventions have their origin in the family values, but do we wish to live by them for the rest of our life? Do they reflect who we actually are?

When we are controlled by fashion, we give control to other people. When we follow the dictates of others we are slaves to them and their ever-changing fashion trends. I will end this chapter with quotations that aptly express the effect of fashion on some people. "Those who make their dress a special part of themselves, will, in general, become of no more value than their dress." "It is not only fine feathers that make fine birds," and from Sathya Sai Baba, "Character is the only true ornament."

CHAPTER 34

ANGER AND VIOLENCE

W<small>E ALL WONDER AT THE</small>
steady increase of anger and violence that appears to be
erupting more frequently, both at the personal level and at
the world level, between individuals and between nations.

Aggression is another pattern of behavior that repeats itself in some families from one generation to the successive
ones. Some children seem to bring their own anger with
them when they are born, as if attracted to a family where
anger is strongly expressed. However, as with all the other
patterns of behavior we have been reviewing, children in a
particular family will tend to react in different ways from
one another. Some will follow the example of an angry
parent while others will be so traumatized that they will vow
never to give vent to anger, and they become too passive or
repressed. Unless the tendency to be angry is faced and resolved it will be suppressed, and at some time when they
have been pushed too far by someone or some event, the
suppressed anger will erupt unexpectedly and out of character, to the intense embarrassment of the angry person.

There is a common saying that illustrates this reaction: "The worm will turn."

Many people struggle valiantly with their aggressive tendencies, even to the point of hating and despising themselves for exhibiting such an objectionable trait, thus turning the anger onto themselves, which is equally damaging. Sathya Sai Baba has been reported as saying that a bout of anger uses up the energy derived from eating three months' ingestion of food. It is extremely debilitating to those who express it, but, not only does it harm the one who is angry; it is equally damaging to all those who are the butt of this aggressive behavior. Children often admit that they live in fear of incurring the anger of either parent and will do almost anything to avoid attracting it, thereby inhibiting their natural spontaneity.

It is difficult for either the one who expresses anger or the one who suppresses it, to be rid of this destructive behavior. Unless we erase the climate of anger in which we were raised, we are most likely to be controlled by it in some fashion and be helpless to avoid it.

Some authorities assert that anger can be an inherited characteristic, but actually, the origin is not important. It remains as control and aggression whether it is inherited or acquired, and often too much time and energy is expended on solving this question that could be better spent on eradicating its influence.

When someone tells me that anger is a problem and there is a genuine desire to deal with this trait, I always ask what patterns were brought into the family circle by each of the parents from their separate family settings. As with all the other aspects of the overall atmosphere present in a family, these original patterns will affect the children born into that family, and its various members will each react in a different way to the energy of anger. When we are able to detach from these repeated patterns and actually destroy the symbol that represents this type of reaction, we will be freeing, not only ourselves and our own family, but also part of the overall thought form around anger at the world level. This will clear the atmosphere that is sometimes almost tangible in certain locations and in some people. As we clear these negative thought forms from the world, they will cease to control those people who have keyed in to them and fed them with their own anger, thus perpetuating anger as a toxic threat to world peace and loving-kindness.

I have witnessed the result of this clearing and the positive affect on the members of a family in which this negative behavior was rampant. It is most fulfilling to be able to free our family and ourselves, for in so doing, we relieve the world of some of the violence that we see all around us. In the personal sense, chapter 39 (anger) and chapter 40 (fear) will help people look at how to work through patches of anger that come from an overly aggressive home environment.

Chapter 35

Patience

Patience is the ability and willingness to wait until the time is right to put into action an idea or plan. Most people are impatient. We want to be given answers now. Things should work out according to our own ideas of when the time is right. But this approach is not always realistic. It is often like picking an apple from a tree when it may look ripe, but it can cause severe stomach cramps if it is eaten while it is still too green. Similarly, if we wait too long and pick it when it is starting to spoil or is overripe, it will cause a different yet equally disturbing distress. We have to accept the timing of the Hi C, which is always correct, instead of insisting on our own faulty timing. Then the "apple" will be just ripe and will cause us no discomfort.

The Hi C approach to timing has to be learned, since most people were not reared with this concept. Most of us have been brought up by parents who have themselves been given a faulty attitude to time by their parents. For instance, one or both parents may have had parents who were always in a hurry, a situation that is becoming common. This is especially the case when both parents work in situations beyond their control. They carry a heavy load of responsibility which often leaves them with insufficient time and energy to devote to their children. The children from such a background react to this situation in various ways. One child may copy the parents by mimicking their behavior of always being in a hurry, and eventually passing on this habit to their own children. Other children may resist always being hurried and will develop the habit of purposely being tardy, in order to assert their independence. However, neither of these habits expresses the real person. Each is a role that was assumed according to the early programming.

Only when we ask the Hi C to indicate the correct timing and are willing to adhere to Its advice can we feel secure in knowing that we are at the right place at the right time. Then we neither try to control others nor allow them to control us. This more balanced approach is possible only if we really are willing to ask the Hi C to guide us. When we do so, we are able to relax and follow Its inner direction. Often we discover that even if we arrive for an appointment too early or too late, it will still be correct, for in many cases, the person we were to meet will also be either early or late.

Being willing to consult the Hi C in this way is the only effective way two people who live together or work as partners can arrive at a point of mutual agreement and adjustment where neither controls the other.

PART V

PATCHES OF KARMA

CHAPTER 36

PRIDE AND VANITY AS PATCHES

According to the dictionary, pride heads the list of the seven deadly or capital sins, and is the only one attributed to the angels, specifically Satan, the fallen angel. Its meaning is conceit or vanity, expressed in exaggerated self-esteem or an overwelming opinion of the importance of one's own ego. Of all the negative emotions, it is the most successful in separating us from the Hi C, which is of equal value in everyone. So how can pride be justified when, by its very definition, it separates and exaggerates the value of the ego over the Hi C?

Pride projects the message that we consider ourselves in some way superior to others and feel proud of our own qualities, gifts, achievements, position, possessions, heritage, children, and a host of other possibilities. We have all heard the phrase "puffed up with pride" applied to a person with an inflated ego, and the charming little fable about the frog who puffed himself up in a desperate effort to be bigger than all the other frogs in the pond only to burst in the effort. Baba often repeats one of his succinct sayings to teach this lesson, "Don't be puffed up with pride or deflated by failure. Accept with equanimity all the pairs of opposites; acceptance or rejection, limelight or shadow."

When have you felt in some way superior to someone else? In what areas is pride operating: physically, mentally, emotionally, or spiritually? Are we proud of our physical attributes, such as a beautiful face, hair, figure, strength, physique, or prowess in sports? But, we have seen that we are not the body. It is like the house in which the Real Self resides as a temporary shelter. So it is foolish to identify with it. In that case, what is the point in having pride about it?

Pride is also attached to material objects that are connected to our physical bodies. These include money, clothes, jewelry, food, cars, houses and all the other innumerable possessions that can cause us to feel superior to those who don't have these possessions. Another possibility is that we are proud of our mental superiority—intellectual achievements, such as degrees, talents, career, or creative abilities. Or are we attached to our popularity and the fact that people like us; or to our generosity, compassion, honesty, unselfishness, our ability to love? All of these are admirable qualities, but if they are the cause of pride, it reduces their true value. Is pride attached to our spiritual achievements or progress? Do we pride ourselves on our spirituality and disparage others who follow other paths? Do we let pride creep in when we give some kind of service to those in need? True compassion springs from a desire to relieve the suffering of others, not to enhance our own value or to impress others.

How can we let go of pride? First we can choose a colored card on which to note instances of it manifesting in our daily life, which will help us to catch sight of it in action.

Then the process is the same as for the other negative emotions. A symbol must be found to represent pride. The method of modeling or drawing the symbol with the conscious mind completely involved in some engrossing occupation is the first step. The symbol is then visualized in the circle opposite your own in the Figure Eight Exercise, and practiced for at least two weeks. At the end of this time, the symbol should be destroyed mentally, and the drawing or model also be destroyed, to impress this message on the subconscious.

Chapter 37

Jealousy and Envy as Patches

J EALOUSY AND ENVY ARE often confused because they are frequently connected. Though they do share the same root causes of greed and selfishness, they are actually quite distinct and different.

Jealousy can become activated when we are attracted to something or someone and are so fearful of losing it that we jealously guard it against loss or theft, and look with suspicion and antagonism at anyone who might try to take it away.

Envy, on the other hand, can be aroused when we see that someone else owns something that we ourselves desire. It easily leads to anger and malice toward another person.

Both emotions are closely linked to the ego and the concept of "me" and "mine." It is obvious that if we hold on tightly to whatever we possess, or crave what belongs to someone else, the last thing we are willing to do is to share it with someone, even someone less fortunate. It makes no difference whether the object of our affection is money, love, food, time, energy, knowledge, or a favorite possession.

It is interesting to observe that children instinctively express jealousy and envy, as both are linked to survival. All young creatures need and seek the necessary food, love, and protection from their parents to ensure their growth into maturity. With the arrival of a sibling or rival for the parents' attention, jealousy and envy invariably erupt, often accompanied by resentment of the intruder into their erstwhile secure world. Such a reaction can lead to hate and so-called crimes of passion.

If a child is given adequate love and security by the parents or other guardians, these twin negative emotions can be nipped in the bud. In this way, they will be prevented from developing into full-blown problems that are difficult to eradicate once they have been allowed to take root in a person's life and have become habitual modes of behavior. Both jealousy and envy cause extreme physical, emotional, and mental stress in a person who is helpless in their grip.

Imagine you are clutching tightly in your hand something that you value highly. Now imagine someone trying to take it away from you. Even the thought of such a situation can cause all your muscles to contract from the tension. Likewise, if you see someone who possesses something you ardently desire, you may feel a strong urge to reach out and aggressively snatch it for yourself. In both of these cases it is love of the possession, whether it is an object or person, that motivates the negative behavior, instead of love for the Hi C.

As with anger, it is helpful to jot down on a card of the chosen color, which is usually yellow for jealousy and green for envy, any incidents during the day that stir up either of these two negative reactions as soon as it occurs. Then ask yourself what or who are you so jealously protecting, or what it is that you crave that belongs to someone else.

To detach from both these emotions, find a symbol to represent them (one at a time) and practice the Figure Eight (page 92) for at least two weeks. Then destroy the symbol, as you did for anger, not forgetting, in addition, to draw the symbol and destroy it to give an even stronger message to the subconscious that you do, indeed, want to be rid of this reaction and the control it has over you. Then using the Maypole (page 9), ask the Hi C to give you what you need to fill you with the opposite emotion of love, concern, caring, or compassion for other people. At the same time ask the Hi C, by using the Hour Glass (page 165), to send you whatever It knows you need. Again making use of the Maypole, ask forgiveness from anyone of whom you have been jealous or envious and direct it to them.

CHAPTER 38

GREED AS A PATCH

GREED IS THE BASIS of most of our other attachments and negative emotions. It is the essence of the ego-based attitude of "me" and "mine." Instead of "Thy will not mine," it is a case of "My will, not Thine or anyone else's," and is a symptom of an extreme need for control by the ego. It is desire carried to the extreme limit; it is an excessive or inordinate desire to acquire more than we need or deserve.

Greedy people are like a bottomless pit. The more they have, the more they want; yet they are never satisfied, whether the desire is for food, drink, money, possessions, love and attention, or fame and fortune. The list is endless.

Greed has as its basis extreme insecurity and the mistaken belief that material things can fill the inner void. In greedy people the greater the insecurity, the more greed is manifested in a desperate attempt to assuage the inner hunger. But since tangible objects are not lasting, they can never completely or permanently satisfy the need. They merely breed even greater insecurity, the very condition they are expected to eliminate. It becomes obvious that the entire process is self-perpetuating.

Greed is the epitome of waste, as it compels us to crave for more of something than we can possibly use; and anything that is not used by its owner could benefit someone else who is being prevented from using it. Here we can choose a card of some other color on which to write the instances of greed of which we have become aware during the day. What do we find we are wanting in excessive amounts that we cannot possibly use? Or what are we holding on to too tightly rather than allowing someone else to make use of? We all tend fiercely to protect those things to which we are the most attached. It helps to watch for strong reactions as we ask ourselves the above questions, as they can lead directly to those areas we most need to see more clearly before we can remedy the situation.

It all comes down to a misconception of where our security lies. Many people seek security in the things themselves, such as their parents, husband or wife, a job, or their own ability or expertise. But all of these and many more are only temporary, and for that very reason they cannot provide the desired security. Our only true and permanent security is in the Hi C, for It knows exactly what we need for our learning and growth.

What symbol is fitting to put in the other circle of the Figure Eight (page 92) to stop the control of greed in preparation to detaching from it? It has been compared to a tapeworm that voraciously devours what its host eats, leaving its benefactor unsatisfied and perpetually hungry, no matter how much is consumed. In that respect it is similar to a parasite that feeds on its host, so see what symbol comes to your mind to represent it, and after at least two weeks of practicing the Figure Eight, destroy the symbol in whatever way appeals to you, but make sure every part of it is demolished.

As with other negative emotions or habits, the habit has to be replaced by an opposite positive one. So what is the opposite of greed? Is it generosity, a willingness to share, concern for others? Each of us will have different ideas, but whatever they may be, ask the Hi C to supply it as you use the Maypole (page 9) and breathe it in deeply and breathe out the greed from the patch from the past.

CHAPTER 39

ANGER AS A PATCH

Anger is one of the most destructive emotions. It is destructive for the one who expresses it, as well as for those to whom it is directed. Baba has said that one outburst of anger uses up the energy derived from the food we eat over a three-month period of time. In that case, it makes sense to eradicate the urge to express anger, and better still, to see what causes us to feel angry in the first place.

When you become aware that you are angry about something, trace that feeling back to the thwarted desire that caused the angry outburst. Write briefly on a red card what triggered it, to whom it was directed, if that applies, and the unfulfilled desire at the base of this reaction.

At the end of each day you can review the list and add any further feelings of anger that were overlooked or repressed. A pattern will begin to emerge that can reveal the most common causes of anger—which will be different from some people and similar to others.

It is most important to be as honest as possible for your own sake, remembering that both the subconscious and the Hi C are completely aware of the past as well as the present, including those aspects of which we are still unconscious. It is also important to know that the Hi C does not criticize, but only encourages us when we allow It to guide us.

There is no need to rush with this process, as it is of prime importance that it be undertaken conscientiously, so it is best to proceed slowly and with care, always asking the Hi C for help along the way.

The next step is to find a symbol to represent the unwanted emotion. For instance, you can ask yourself what it feels like, or where in your body it is lodged. It may feel like a ball of fire located in your chest or stomach, or elsewhere in your body, or like an angry-looking mask, or a clenched fist. Ask the Hi C to show you a suitable symbol, or resort to the method of drawing or modeling one, as described earlier. The Figure Eight (page 92) should be practiced for at least two weeks, using the symbol for anger in the circle opposite your own.

There are many different ways to destroy symbols for such unwanted control factors. Many people favor burning them, others choose to drop them in an imaginary vat of acid, still others prefer to throw them over a cliff, into a volcano, or they hurl them into outer space.

In addition to the imaginary destruction, it is important to draw the symbol on a sheet of paper, which can then also be destroyed. This gives a strong clear message to the subconscious that you are serious about detaching from this negative emotion.

It is essential to fill the space which the symbol for anger occupied with a positive emotion. What would be the opposite of anger as an antidote? Using the Maypole (page 9), take a ribbon and ask to be given whatever was indicated as a replacement for the anger. Breathe in deeply whatever that is, and breathe out any remaining remnants of anger.

In addition, if the anger was directed to a person, it will be necessary to ask that person for forgiveness, and direct the love from the Hi C to him or her to heal the wound you inflicted by your anger.

As you persevere with this daily exercise you will become aware of a steady improvement for fewer episodes will be noted on your red card. You may also notice that the bouts of anger will be less severe and of shorter duration. In dealing with all of these emotions, it is important to remain aware that you are not competing with anyone other than your own self.

CHAPTER 40

FEAR AS A PATCH

Fear is, perhaps, the most crippling of all the negative emotions, as expressed by such sayings as, "I was paralyzed by fear," or "Fear held him helpless in its grip," and, "She fainted dead away with fear." Fear is directly connected to desire. We either fear that what we want will not materialize, or, on the other hand, that what we do not want will come to pass.

Fear is also extremely infectious. It ignites the "fight or flight" reaction in the solar plexus. Animals are reputed to be able to smell when it is operating near humans, as well as near other animals. As soon as a fearful situation is detected, it spreads like wildfire through an entire herd, causing them to stampede without knowing what they are madly escaping. A similar reaction can occur in a crowd of people. All that is needed is for one person to express fear, or utter one fear-arousing word (such as "Fire!") and the fear thus evoked will spread rapidly through the crowd, causing them to act like a flock of sheep, blindly following the leader.

On the other hand, in the right place and at the right time, fear can be very useful to signal a warning of approaching danger, which can then be either avoided or faced. In that case, it leads to positive action, such as the "flight or fight" reaction, expressed in such sayings as, "Fear lent wings to his feet," and, "Fear gave him the strength of ten men."

On the negative side, fear can be used to gain control over other people. People who seek to wield power over another can achieve it more easily if they can discover that person's fears. They will be able to play on this person until the victim is cowed and becomes subservient. A snake arouses fear in a rabbit that becomes as if frozen in its tracks and unable to escape. It is then a simple matter for the snake to pounce on it and gulp it down.

We are all born with three basic fears: loud noise, being dropped, and being left alone. Therefore, we all experience fear, but some fears have been so strong that they are repressed. They lie so deeply buried in the subconscious that we are unaware of them until something triggers them unexpectedly, when they erupt and overwhelm us. So, the first step is to identify our own fears.

Fear falls into three categories. There is general fear of war, earthquakes, fire, floods, hurricanes, drought, hunger, and other disasters. Then there are common fears shared by many people individually, such as fear of death, failure, destitution, loss of a job, loss of a loved one, rejection, and many others. Lastly, there are fears that are not necessarily shared by the majority of people, such as fear of the dark, fear of change, fear of the unknown, fear of snakes, spiders, or mice, to name but a few.

Because fear attracts to itself what we most fear, it is essential to relinquish it and replace it with its opposite emotion, which is love, as in the saying, "Perfect love casts out all fear."

Take a card and write down any fears that attract your attention. This is the first step in detaching from it.

Exercise 8, the Jack (or Star) to remove fear, can be used to dispel this condition. In addition, practicing the Figure Eight around a suitable symbol, followed by eliminating it, should also be done.

It has been said that there is nothing to fear but fear itself, so as soon as we remove the fear, we can work on the patch that we brought with us as one of the lessons we still need to learn.

EXERCISE 8
THE JACK (OR STAR) TO ERADICATE FEAR

Let your mind go back to a recent time when you experienced a specific fear. Allow yourself to relive it, but observe where in your body you are feeling it. For instance, is it like a lump in your throat, a sinking feeling in your stomach, a tightness in your solar plexus, or discomfort at some other site?

What does it remind you of—a hot coal, an ice cube, a prickly burr, or some other symbol?

Imagine you are reaching up above your head and taking hold of a jack (like those used in a children's game in the USA) or a three-dimensional star. Whichever symbol you choose will be composed of light, and the points are like rays of light.

Pull it down as if it were on a pulley, like some lamps suspended from the ceiling. Let it stop about six inches (15 cm) away from your body, in line with your solar plexus or diaphragm.

As you breathe out, let go of the symbol of fear from the part of your body where you located it. It will be magnetically drawn into the middle of the jack (or star), which will, like a "black hole," negate it.

As you breathe in, inhale the light emanating from the spokes of the jack to replace the fear which you have just expelled, and to heal the old trauma that caused it.

Repeat the breathing rhythm with the same fear for not more than 5 minutes at a time.

Push the jack (star) back up above your head on the pulley, ready for the next time you may need it.

It can be used whenever you are aware of feeling fear, and as many times during the day as necessary, but not for more than 5 minutes at a time.

Epilogue

All of these suggestions may seem to involve too much hard work, but you don't need to detach from all the patches of your quilt at the same time. Everyone has brought different patches on which to work during this present life. It may not be possible to discard all of them in this one lifetime. In fact, that might not even be advisable to try to accomplish. Only those that have attracted you to the opportunity to learn from them will need to be de-energized and removed this time. You can pick one, or one will announce itself.

Yes, it requires hard work in order to be free, but what better way to use your time and energy than by working through old karma and allowing the Hi C to live through you so that you do not incur any more karma? It is very much like paying off all your debts by working hard to earn the necessary money to be free from the burden that you have been carrying around for many lifetimes.

So far, we have looked at the patches we have all brought with us that form our patchwork quilt and allow us to use up the energy that they still retain so we can discard them. This entails making a conscious decision followed by action in the form of practicing the Figure Eight to help to reduce the control that negative habits have held over us. After two or more weeks of practicing it, we can detach from the symbol that represents each of these aspects and destroy it.

But we also need to develop positive traits to replace the negative ones. These could include honesty, patience, caring and compassion, humility, the ability to share, or giving service to those less fortunate than ourselves, and many others. We each will have a different list, as we have all brought with us some positive aspects as well as less desirable ones, so we have to determine what we are lacking in our makeup. Then we can use the Maypole and the Hour Glass to ask the Hi C to supply them and be willing to breathe them in and let go of any control over us.

As soon as we start on this course of action, it becomes an adventure, and we will discover that all kinds of help from most unexpected sources will come to aid us in this endeavor.

This present time in history, when everything is so accelerated, is actually the perfect time to be engaged in this crucial task. With the daily help of the Hi C and our surrender to Its will, we can all work on freeing ourselves to be Its instruments. What more could we ask for in this lifetime and in the new millennium? So, let us all work on this task which will automatically help to free the world. And let us stop wasting our precious time and energy and take advantage of the golden opportunity available to all of us to seek within for the help and guidance of the Hi C and ask It to think, feel, speak, and act and love through each of us every day.

INDEX

Phyllis Krystal, born in England, is a practicing psychotherapist who has developed a unique approach to therapy using symbols and visualization techniques to help clients detach from external authority figures and patterns. She teaches people to rely on their own Higher Consciousness as guide and teacher. Phyllis lectures in the United States, Europe, Australia, New Zealand, and Tazmania. She is also a devotee of Satya Sai Baba, the world-renowned avatar living in India, whose teachings and personal influence offer her inspiration in her own work. Phyllis has written several best-selling books, including *Cutting the Ties That Bind, Cutting More Ties That Bind, Reconnecting the Love Energy, Sai Baba: The Ultimate Experience,* and *Taming Our Monkey Mind*—all published by Weiser.